3

D0930854

OFFICIALLY WITHDRAWN
NEW HAVEN FREE PUBLIC LIBRARY

OCT 8 2 2002

What Manner of Man

What Manner of Man

 Johnson Publishing Company, Inc.
Chicago: 1976

FREE PUBLIC LIBRARY
NEW HAVEN, CT 06510

a biography of

Martin Luther King, Jr.

by Lerone Bennett, Jr.

with an introduction by Benjamin E. Mays

Copyright © 1964 and 1968 by Johnson
Publishing Company, Inc.
Second edition, revised and enlarged, 1965
Third revised edition, 1968
Fourth revised edition, 1976
Fifth revised edition, 1981
Sixth revised edition, 1986
Seventh revised edition, 1989
Eighth revised edition, 1992
Ninth Printing, 2000

All rights reserved, including the right to reproduce
this book or portions thereof in any form.

Library of Congress Cataloging in Publication Data

Bennett, Lerone Jr., 1928-
What Manner of Man: A biography of Martin Luther King, Jr.
With an introd. by Benjamin E. Mays.
ISBN 0-87485-027-4
King, Martin Luther, Jr., 1929-1968.
Afro-Americans—Biography.
Baptists—United States—Clergy—Biography

E185.97.K5 B4 1976
323.4'092'4   83-189238

PRINTED IN THE USA

To my children

Joy, Constance and Courtney,
and Lerone III

and to the future of their generation in
whom the dreams and struggles outlined
here will find fulfillment

INTRODUCTION

Both the author and Dr. King are graduates of Morehouse College, were schoolmates, and both received their college degrees from my hand. It is appropriate, therefore, that I write a brief introduction to the book, *What Manner of Man*.

Although there was no doubt in my mind that both would succeed in life, being the kind of students they were, I was not wise enough to say to what extent. Both have gone far in an exceptionally short time—one as a journalist and author; the other as a Nobel Prize winner and the chief exponent of the doctrine of non-violence. Both were nurtured in the Morehouse tradition, which says to the student silently and firmly, "You are expected to do well at Morehouse and in the world." Not all Morehouse men do well, but this challenge is an important force in developing men at Morehouse and was a motivating factor in shaping the future of Bennett and King.

The book is well named, even though it is hardly possible for anyone to explain what it is that makes a man great and especially one who belongs to a submerged group subjected to denials and embarrassed by indignities.

Many potentially able men are never given a chance to rise to greatness. Most men cannot rise beyond the ordinary. Although there are millions of Americans, only a negligible number can attain to the Presidency of the United States, a position in which opportunity, responsibility, and time determine the extent to which a President can successfully meet the challenges that confront him during his four or eight years in office. The truly great American Presidents are few indeed.

It may be that only one man in ten million could have led the Montgomery boycott without that city exploding into one of the worst race riots in history. I had offered young King a position on the faculty at Morehouse, but he wanted to try pastoring. If he had accepted my offer, he might never have developed into the kind of man that he is. If Rosa Parks had behaved as Negroes in Montgomery and in the South were supposed to behave—get up and let a white man have her seat—the Montgomery Improvement Association would hardly have been organized. If the organization had chosen a person other than King to communicate the Negroes' grievances to the city fathers, Dr. King might have gone through life as a successful Baptist preacher and no more. His rare ability to lead and inspire the classes as well as the masses, in a crusade for social justice, might never have been called forth.

But he was thrust into leadership at a crucial moment in the history of the city of Montgomery—perhaps in the history of the United States. The time and the right man met. Here young King had to draw upon all that he had learned and read at Morehouse, Crozer, and Boston University; all that he had absorbed from Christ, Gandhi, and other nonviolent writers; and all that he had gained through meditation and prayer. Only an exceptional mind, a rare spirit, and an abiding faith could have enabled Dr. King to be absolutely fearless and absolutely nonviolent, in jail and out, when stabbed and threatened, with his home and family constantly harassed and at one time in danger of being destroyed by bombs.

To some, the rise of Martin Luther King, Jr., to world renown is just an accident. To others, it is the divine hand. In this readable and fascinating book, the author, Lerone Bennett, tells the story of a true American, a true Christian hero.

Benjamin E. Mays

Morehouse College
Atlanta, Georgia

AUTHOR'S PREFACE

This is an interim assessment of a man and the mood he mediates.
Martin Luther King's youth and his continuing development as a
man and as a national leader preclude a more definitive study, which
must, of necessity, await the unfolding of events. King's pervasive influence, however, justifies an interim assessment; and his thirty-fifth
year and the awarding of the Nobel Peace Prize offer convenient
vantage points for such an assessment.

To a great extent, I have relied here on material collected in personal
interviews with Dr. King, his wife, close friends, classmates, and
relatives. I have also drawn on my personal recollections of Morehouse
College, where I was a student from 1945 to 1949, and Atlanta,
Georgia, where I lived and worked from 1945 to 1953. I have also had
the benefit of an extended study of the voluminous Johnson Publishing
Company files, which contain speeches, newspaper clips, articles,
programs, confidential memoranda, etc., covering every facet of King's
life. Additional information and suggestions came from Robert E.
Johnson, a college classmate of Martin Luther King; John H. Britton,

who covered the Birmingham demonstrations; Alvin C. Adams, who interviewed Dr. King, Mrs. King, and other members of the family in the fall of 1963; and Dr. Howard Thurman, a pioneer advocate of nonviolence who visited Gandhi in 1935. All students of King's life are, of course, indebted to Lawrence D. Reddick, whose excellent study, *Crusader Without Violence*, carried King through 1958.

In the reduction of the great mass of material to paper, I have been aided immeasurably by many people: Publisher John H. Johnson, who provided facilities and time for the organization and writing of the book; Doris E. Saunders, who produced the book, selected the photographs and offered valuable advice and suggestions; Ariel Strong, who played an important role at every stage as an organizer and checker of facts, figures, and style; Herbert Temple, who designed the book jacket; Lucille Phinnie, who searched out elusive dates and other research information; and Savannah Caldwell, the efficient secretary of the Book Division. My wife Gloria helped greatly; so also did Mrs. Coretta Scott King and the staff of the Southern Christian Leadership Conference. Most of all, I am indebted to Dr. King whose books, particularly *Stride Toward Freedom* and *Why We Can't Wait*, are invaluable source material. Without the help of these and other people, this book could not have been published. I alone, of course, am responsible for limitations of style, articulation, and organization.

The title of this book is an excerpt from a famous Biblical quotation. It is used here in a symbolic sense as an invocation of a man who moves not natural elements but social forces and millions of human beings.

Lerone Bennett, Jr.

October, 1964

CONTENTS

ILLUSTRATIONS

What Manner of Man

Soil

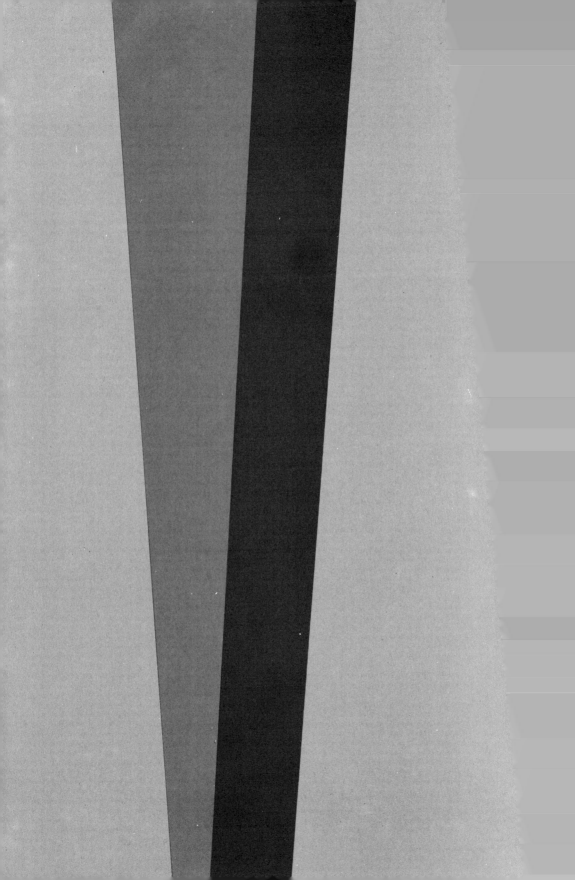

THE SCENE and the encounter were arresting.

Face to face stood Mohandas K. Gandhi and a group of American Negro pilgrims. Gandhi regarded his Negro visitors with interest. He had a deep and empathic interest in the American Negro. Many years before this meeting, in 1929, he had sent a message of greeting to the Negroes of America:

> Let not the 12 million Negroes be ashamed of the fact that they are the grandchildren of slaves. There is no dishonour in being slaves. There is dishonour in being slave-owners. But let us not think of honour or dishonour in connection with the past. Let us realize that the future is with those who would be truthful, pure and loving. For, as the old wise men have said, truth ever is, untruth never was. Love alone binds and truth and love accrue only to the truly humble.

Since the publication of this message in the July, 1929, *Crisis*, scores of Negro Americans had made pilgrimages to Gandhi's home. Now, in 1935, he was being honored by the presence of another admiring group. For several minutes, Gandhi and his guests discussed Christianity, oppression, and love. Then, unexpectedly, Gandhi asked the American Negroes to sing one of his favorite songs, "Were You There When They Crucified My Lord?" The old sad words rose and swelled like a benediction, like a curse, like a prayer, the more terrible, the more poignant perhaps for the strange setting.

> *Were you there when they crucified my Lord?*
> *Were you there when they nailed him to the tree?*
> *Oh, sometimes, it causes me to tremble, tremble, tremble.*
> *Were you there when they crucified my Lord?*

The words, weighed down with centuries of accepted and transmuted sorrow, winged their way to Gandhi's heart, and Gandhi lived through the words to the experience the words mediated, to the centuries on centuries of suffering and strife and to the attempts of a disinherited people to wrest from life some grain of dignity via the ancient and primitive ideology of saying yes and meaning no, of resisting—and surviving—by not resisting. When, at last, the words were done, Gandhi sat for a moment, silent. Then he said: "Perhaps it will be through the Negro that the unadulterated message of nonviolence will be delivered to the world."

Twenty-one years later, Martin Luther King, Jr., who was six when Gandhi spoke, fleshed out, in pain and in love, Gandhi's prophecy and Gandhi's hope. And King's act, though focused by the act of the brown man of India, grew out of, exfoliated from, the polarities of pain and joy that Gandhi sensed in the subsoil of the Negro soul. King's genius—and it was that, precisely—was not in the application of Gandhism to the Negro struggle but in the transmuting of Gandhism by grafting it onto the only thing that could give it relevance and force in the Negro community, the Negro religious tradition. In the process, King rose to new heights of creative leadership, perceiving not only what was "ripe for development" but *creating* new fruit for the sun of despair to ripen. In so doing, in lifting men's eyes to the ancient hope of a world where men will beat their swords into ploughshares and

their arrows into pruning hooks, Martin Luther King, Jr., became perhaps the greatest leader in the history of the Negro protest and one of
the great spiritual leaders of mankind.

No one could have predicted at his birth or for twenty-six years
thereafter that King would pass this social miracle. King, like Gandhi,
was born without fanfare in comfortable, rigorously conventional circumstances. He was born in 1929 in Atlanta, a city haunted by the Negro and the Negro cause. The mark of the Negro was seared into
Atlanta's soul by William Tecumseh Sherman, the Civil War general
who burned the town in his famous march to the sea. Thereafter, the
Negro, and the Negro cause, would never be far from Atlanta's eyes.
From Atlanta, in the 1880's, Henry Grady, the white Southern orator,
marched North as a missionary of (white) North-South reconciliation
on a program of peaceful and permanent subordination of the Negro
population. To Atlanta, in 1895, came Booker T Washington, the
flawed Negro leader, with a parable of the empty bucket and a meta-
phor of the open hand. ("In all things that are purely social, we can be
as separate as the fingers, yet one as the hand in all things essential to
mutual progress.") From Atlanta, W. E. B. Du Bois launched, in the
dawn of the twentieth century, the anti-Washington movement that
led to the founding of the National Association for the Advancement
of Colored People. Here, in a lush setting of magnolias, peach trees,
and dogwood blossoms, Walter White, the NAACP leader, was born.
And here also Martin Luther King, Jr., breathed for the first time the
air of life. King was born at a forking point of worlds. Ten months
after his birth, the Western world collapsed in a calamitous depression.
But this was visible to no one in January, 1929, least of all to Martin
Luther King, Sr., whose attention was focused on the impending birth
of his second child.

King the elder was a great brown oak of a man, the pastor of a small
church and a student at Atlanta's Morehouse College. In 1929, he and
his wife, Alberta, and their one-year-old daughter, Christine, lived in
the home of his father-in-law, a tall, dark, strong-willed pastor named
Adam Daniel Williams. The Kings and the Williamses occupied separate apartments in a big (twelve rooms) two-story house on Auburn Avenue. Auburn Avenue, then and now, occupied a position in
the Negro community similar to the Wall Street of the white community. The street, in the heart of downtown Atlanta, dropped precipi-

tously from Peachtree Street, the white folks' street, into a valley which contained some of the largest Negro-owned businesses in America, the Atlanta Life Insurance Company, the *Atlanta World*, and the Citizens Trust Company, which later became the only Negro bank in the Federal Reserve System. Rising from this valley of high finance and Black Puritan industry, Auburn Avenue climbed to a hill of fine churches, including Ebenezer Baptist Church, and a residential section of large, small, and indifferent homes. On this crest, at 501 Auburn Avenue, was the white and gray frame house King and his family shared with in-laws. In 1929, the house set back off the street a little, withdrawn in modesty, and in pride.

Inside this house, in the first weeks of 1929, all was tension and anxiety. Men and women bustled to and fro. Visitors spoke in hushed tones. Kettles of water steamed in the kitchen.

Tension rose alarmingly on January 14 and reached a peak on Tuesday, January 15. On that cold, gray morning, King the elder walked the floor, his mind focused on his wife Alberta, who had had an unusually difficult time with the baby she was carrying. She lay now in a downstairs room where, after hours of agony and heavy doses of sedation, she gave birth to a male child. For a brief moment, all hearts stopped, for it seemed that the baby was stillborn. He lay so still, so quiet, that the doctor had to slap his bottom vigorously to bring forth the customary cry of life. Through an error, apparently, the baby born that day was listed officially as Michael Luther King, Jr., and remained so, officially, until 1957 when he received his first passport. But to the father and, later, to the world, the baby was Martin Luther King, Jr.

The fat placid baby who came so unwillingly into the world had deep roots in the soil of Afro-America. Some of his forebears, it is true, came from Ireland and some, the aboriginal Indians, were here when Columbus arrived. Yet, the baby was defined at birth and would be defined later by one of the most violent acts in recorded history, the forcible capture and transporting of millions of Africans from Africa to America. The nameless forebears of Martin Luther King, Jr., were whipped for hundreds of years in the slave quarters of America and were driven, with straps, to the fields. The sun rose and the sun set, day after day, for two hundred years, and the ancestors of Martin Luther King, Jr., were bought, sold, exchanged, violated, like so many cattle.

From this long line of men and women, black, red, and white—nameless but nonetheless important for all that—came the Kings, of Georgia, who were freed in a bloody and violent Civil War. During the Reconstruction period, the Kings voted and participated in the public life of the community as citizens and potential public servants. But year by year they were driven back toward slavery. Thus, in the 1880's, James Albert King, Martin Luther King's paternal grandfather, found himself enmeshed in the tentacles of peonage.

King was a sharecropper on a plantation in Stockbridge, about twenty miles from Atlanta. The white landlord for whom he worked provided him with land, a house, seed, fertilizer, and sometimes food. When the crop was harvested and sold, the profits, theoretically, were divided equally between King and the white landlord. But since King could neither read nor write and since the landlord kept the books, King slipped deeper and deeper into debt, the victim of some horribly tangible and horribly palpable nightmare.

Part Negro and part Irish, James Albert King, in the beginning, was a hard-working sharecropper who dreamed of buying a small farm for his family. But as he sank ever more deeply into debt, he gave up hope and spent his weekends trying to drink himself into forgetfulness. James Albert King's soil, a soil that yielded peasants, paupers, murderers, robbers and, finally, a Martin Luther King, was that soil of sorrow I have described elsewhere. "To work from sun-up to sun-down for a whole year and to end owing 'the man' $400 for the privilege of working; to do this year after year and to sink deeper and deeper into debt; to be chained to the land by bills at the plantation store; to wash away this knowledge with bad gin, to blot it out in an ecstasy of song and prayer; to sing, to pray, to cry . . . to be powerless and to curse one's self for cowardice; to be conditioned by dirt and fear and shame and signs; to become a part of these signs and to feel them in the deepest recess of the spirit . . . to be a plaything of judges and courts and policemen; to be black in a white fire and to believe finally in one's own unworthiness; to be without books and words and pretty pictures; to be without newspapers and radios; to be without *understanding* . . . to give in finally; to bow, to scrape, to grin; and to hate one's self for one's servility and weakness"—all this was a Kafkaian nightmare which James Albert King lived for days and nights and years.

To this sharecropper, in this condition, were born ten children. The child who holds our attention, the male child who became the father of Martin Luther King, Jr., was born on December 19, 1899, and spent the first sixteen years of his life on the Stockbridge plantation. It seems that King's mother and father disagreed on his name, the father insisting on Martin Luther and the mother holding out for Michael Luther. The disagreement was never really settled. No one knew then that it would be important later. As a result, King's father was known as Michael Luther or "Mike" until he was twenty-two. Hence, the original confusion about the name of his son.

King the father was an ambitious, sensitive, hot-tempered youth who came early to indignation. Going one day to visit his mother, Delia, a dark, attractive woman who washed and ironed for a white woman who lived in a red-brick house, King came face to face with the problem that would consume his life and the life of his oldest son. The white children of the house invited him to lunch, but their mother shut the door in his face and directed him to the rear, where a sandwich was pushed through the partially-opened door. King looked at the sandwich and then looked at the white woman. Through the door, he could see his mother ironing the white people's clothes. All of a sudden, something snapped inside him. He threw the sandwich on the ground and ran home, telling himself as he went: "One of these days I'm going to have a brick house, and my brick house is going to be as fine as any brick house."

A second incident steeled his determination. When he was twelve or so, he went with his father to settle accounts with the white landlord. The landlord consulted his books and announced that James Albert King's cotton crop for that year balanced to the penny his debts. Young King, who was something of an expert in mathematics at the dilapidated plantation school, spoke up. "Papa," he asked, "what about the cotton seed?" Young King, his mind running on ahead of the adults, had perceived that if the cotton canceled his father's debts then the cotton seed, which both adults had forgotten, would bring some $1,000 in clear money. This fact, and young King's "uppityness" enraged the landlord, who asked: "What you got your mouth in it for?" He lifted his foot to kick the boy, but James Albert King interceded, promising that he would "take care" of his son.

It was not too long after this incident that King decided that he had had enough of the plantation. Throwing his shoes across his back, he started walking toward Atlanta, still dreaming of the red-brick house he would own one day. In Atlanta, King worked days, saved his money, and studied at night. By extraordinary industry, he completed high school and entered a local college, Morehouse. During this same period, he branched out as a fervent Baptist preacher. Within a short time, he was pastor of two small Atlanta churches. While still a student, the young man met, wooed, and married Alberta Williams, the calm and comely daughter of A. D. Williams, one of the leading pastors of the city. This, as it turned out, was an ideal match. King's father-in-law, Adam Daniel Williams, was a keen-witted pioneer who was unusually successful in accumulating worldly goods and diffusing the spiritual insights of the Negro religious tradition. In 1894, the year before Booker T. Washington made his famous "Atlanta Compromise" address, Williams had taken over a debt-ridden Atlanta church. Within a few years, the steel-willed patriarch had made Ebenezer Baptist Church one of the strongest institutions of its kind.

The aging pastor was an excellent judge of character, and he was delighted when the young Morehouse student asked for the hand of his daughter. With Williams' blessings, the couple were married on Thanksgiving Day in 1926. They moved immediately into the Williams' home on Auburn. This was considered a temporary arrangement, but it proved so beneficial to all concerned that it was never changed.

After the marriage, Mrs. King, who had attended Spelman Seminary and Hampton Institute, worked as a teacher until the arrival of her first baby, Christine. King returned to his studies at Morehouse College and continued his work as pastor of Travelers Rest Baptist Church. At the insistence of his father-in-law, however, he relinquished his small charge and became assistant pastor at Ebenezer Baptist Church. On the death of the Rev. Mr. Williams in 1931, the young man became pastor of what was by then the family church.

During this period of hope and ambition and growth, both the father and grandfather of Martin Luther King, Jr., were among the pioneer leaders of the modern Negro resistance movement which grew out of and reflected the violent struggles of slave rebels like Gabriel Prosser and Nat Turner, both of whom were King boyhood idols, and the somewhat more successful efforts of Negro and white abolitionists. Negro preachers, men made in the image of King the elder and his father-in-law, were pivotally successful in molding the leadership tradition of this movement, a tradition that stressed lyrical and somewhat effulgent oratory and a cautious, "realistic" approach to the problems of a racial minority which lacked absolute initiative vis-à-vis their oppressors and had to attack therefore with tact and with caution. The limitations of this tradition, its inarticulation with the great masses of Negroes and its reliance on the goodwill and generosity of the oppressors, were, in part, a reflection of the Negro situation, a situation defined by powerlessness. Crucial to an understanding of the leadership heritage Martin Luther King, Jr., inherited—and expanded—is an understanding not of love but of a brute fact of power: minority status maintained by the implacable will of a majority which controlled—and controls—*all* the lines of force. Faced with this brute fact—powerlessness vs. power—Negro leaders have expressed themselves in two dominant patterns: protest and activism. Protest is an *attitude* of non-acceptance based on sustained contention via political and legal tactics *within* the system. Activism, on the other hand, is a program of direct action based on *revolt* on the edges or outside the system. To the right of these patterns of resistance are programs of accommodation (acceptance of the system and the proving of self and race by accumulation, good works, and good behavior), black nationalism (separation from the system), and interracial conciliation (goodwill efforts to effect gradual changes in the system by education, research, exposure, persuasion, etc.)

By 1916, the year King the elder migrated to Atlanta, these approaches had been institutionalized in the Negro community and social types had emerged with life styles embodying the dominant patterns. The major leadership types which could be seen in Atlanta, then and now, were militants who relied on protest methods; accommodators who counselled resignation and hard work; nationalists who called for the creation of a Negro state; and moderates who articulated a *via media* between protest and accommodation.

Throughout the history of American Negroes, the relative weight of leaders embodying the major patterns has waned and waxed with the socio-political fortunes of the Negro masses. King's grandfathers, for example, lived and worked under the shadow of four radically different men—Frederick Douglass, Booker T. Washington, W. E. B. Du Bois, Marcus Garvey—who are generally considered the most talented leaders in the history of Negro resistance. Frederick Douglass, the first great national Negro leader and a boyhood idol of Martin Luther King, Jr., died in 1895, one year after A. D. Williams began his Atlanta pastorate. Douglass, an ex-slave who escaped and became a leading editor, politician, and abolitionist, articulated a program of persistent, manly protest utilizing all weapons, large and small, violent and nonviolent. For fifty years, from 1845 to 1895, Douglass was universally recognized as the leading American Negro. During this span, he hewed out the boundaries and the limitations of the Negro resistance movement, holding aloft, through good years and bad years, a program of total and immediate integration. Although Douglass knew little of India and less of Hegel, he was an early advocate of sit-ins and ride-ins and he stated the Hegelian doctrine of progress-through-struggle with an eloquence and simplicity that would have pleased that latter-day Hegelian, Martin Luther King, Jr. "The whole history of the progress of human liberty," Douglass said in 1857, "shows that all concessions yet made to her august claims, have been born of earnest struggle. . . . If there is no struggle, there is no progress, those who profess to favor freedom and yet deprecate agitation are men who want crops without ploughing up the ground, they want rain without thunder and lightning. They want the ocean without the awful roar of its many waters. This struggle may be a moral one, or it may be a physical one, or it may be both moral and physical, but it must be a struggle. Power concedes nothing without a demand. It never did and it never will. . . . Men may not get all they pay for in this world, but they must certainly pay for all they get. If we are to get free from the oppression and wrongs heaped upon us, we must pay for their removal. We must do this by labor, by suffering, by sacrifice, and if need be, by our lives and the lives of others."

Douglass, who served as Minister to Haiti and Marshal of the District of Columbia in the Reconstruction period, was thrown into the

shade by the post-Reconstruction reaction which pushed King's ancestors back toward slavery. In the year of Douglass' death, Booker T.
Washington, a very different personality, went to Atlanta with a program of appeasement and retreat. In his Atlanta Compromise address
at the Cotton States Exposition of 1895, Washington, the president
of Alabama's Tuskegee Institute, asked Negroes to abandon politics
and pressure tactics and to concentrate on what he called the "essen-
tials," the development of "Christian" (i.e., humble) character and
the accumulation of material possessions. The white power structure
of America, surprised and delighted by this unexpected capitulation,
immediately selected Washington as the new Negro leader, to the disgust of Negro intellectuals like John Hope of Morehouse who said
Washington's program was impractical, unwise, and unmanly.

From the Negro liberal arts colleges of Atlanta, which now became a
center of anti-Washington militancy, came the seeds of the modern
Negro protest movement. In the first decades of the twentieth century,
while A. D. Williams was consolidating his control over Ebenezer
Baptist Church, W. E. B. Du Bois, a young Atlanta University professor, rallied the white liberal and Negro militant forces of America. Du
Bois, who was a familiar and persuasive figure in Atlanta during the
days of King's childhood and adolescence, was the second great leader
of the Negro resistance movement. The acerbic professor, slight, thin,
intense, proposed a program of "ceaseless agitation," involving "the
use of force of every sort: moral suasion, propaganda and where possible even physical resistance." From Atlanta, in June, 1905, Du Bois
issued a call for the first meeting of the germinal Niagara movement
which led by mutations, mergers, and alliances, to the founding of
the National Association for the Advancement of Colored People.
The "call" for the NAACP's first meeting, though issued on Lincoln's birthday in 1909, described with great eloquence the social climate of the world into which Martin Luther King, Jr. was born and
which he would change.

> If Mr. Lincoln could revisit this country in the flesh, he would be
> disheartened and discouraged. He would learn that on January 1, 1901,
> Georgia had rounded out a new confederacy by disfranchising the Ne-
> gro, after the manner of all the other Southern states. He would learn
> that the Supreme Court of the United States, supposedly a bulwark of
> American liberties, had refused every opportunity to pass squarely upon

this disfranchisement of millions, by laws avowedly discriminatory and openly enforced in such manner that the white men may vote and black men be without a vote in their government; he would discover, therefore, that taxation without representation is the lot of millions of wealth-producing American citizens, in whose hands rests the economic progress and welfare of an entire section of the country.

He would learn that the Supreme Court, according to the official statement of one of its own judges in the Berea College case, has laid down the principle that if an individual state chooses, it may "make it a crime for white and colored persons to frequent the same market place at the same time, or appear in an assemblage of citizens convened to consider questions of a public or political nature in which all citizens, without regard to race, are equally interested."

In many states Lincoln would find justice enforced, if at all, by judges elected by one element in a community to pass upon the liberties and lives of another. He would see the black men and women, for whose freedom a hundred thousand of soldiers gave their lives, set apart in trains, in which they pay first-class fares for third-class service, and segregated in railway stations and in places of entertainment; he would observe that state after state declines to do its elementary duty in preparing the Negro through education for the best exercise of citizenship.

The association, which was dominated in the beginning by white liberals, opened the eyes of Negroes to a whole new vista of "respectable protest," of litigation, lobbying, and a propaganda of enlightenment. In the twenties, branches sprang up in all sections of the country, including Atlanta, which became a fount of the "new protest." The "new protest," which frightened some Negroes of that day, seemed inordinately tame to others—among them Asa Philip Randolph, a young labor leader who derided "sterile protest" and called for an opening to the masses. To the right of Randolph, to the right of almost all American Negroes, was Marcus Garvey, a brilliant, bombastic Jamaican who organized the largest black nationalist movement and one of the largest mass movements in the history of Negro resistance. Garvey, like Elijah Muhammad with whom King would clash later, was openly contemptuous of the mainstream militancy of the Negro leadership group. Neither protest nor activism, he said, would alter significantly the social conditions of an oppressed minority living in the midst of a

Birthplace of Martin Luther King, Jr., was two-story
frame house (c.) on Auburn Avenue in Atlanta,
Georgia. At time of King's birth, his parents
shared home with their in-laws.

Mother, Mrs. Alberta King, is former Atlanta
teacher. She is daughter of late A. D. Williams,
who served as pastor of Ebenezer Baptist Church
from 1894 to 1931.

Father, Martin Luther King, Sr., is
Atlanta pastor and leader. He and his
son were copastors of the Ebenezer
Baptist Church (background) which
is near the Auburn Avenue house.

majority which feared and hated them. Raising a banner of black supremacy, Garvey called in the early and middle twenties for a return to
Africa. Though he failed in his ultimate purpose, Garvey evoked an
unprecedented response from the Negro masses, raising in a single two-
year period some ten million dollars, more money than any Negro
leader, before or since, has ever dreamed of. Garvey's success, as Myrdal
noted, told of a dissatisfaction so deep and pervasive in the Negro
ghetto that it bordered on hopelessness of ever gaining a satisfying social life in America.

The hidden springs of Garvey's triumph lay in the changing climate
of the day. With the beginning of the great migration of Negroes to
the North and the urbanization and radicalization of the Negro masses,
a new correlation of forces emerged which placed great strain on
mainstream Negro leadership techniques of litigation and negotiation.
This process, which began in the twenties on the eve of Martin Luther
King's birth, continued throughout the thirties and forties, ripening
the fruit King would pluck in the fifties. But no one could foresee
that development then. Mainstream Negro leadership techniques
seemed entirely adequate to the hour. Indeed, they seemed quite radical in Atlanta, where A. D. Williams, Martin Luther King's grandfather, moved to the forefront as one of the pioneer leaders of the
Atlanta NAACP branch. Williams was a leader of an enraged citizens'
group which forced the city to build a Negro public high school by de-
feating a bond issue that contained no provisions for educational facilities for Negroes. When the Atlanta *Georgian*, a Hearst paper, called
the Negro protesters "dirty and ignorant," Williams took the lead in
organizing a boycott of the paper. It has been estimated that as many
as six thousand Negroes dropped the paper in a single day. The boycott led to the eventual death of the *Georgian*. King's father continued
the family tradition in the thirties and forties, heading the citizens'
committee which instituted Atlanta's first suit for equalization of
teachers' salaries.

Because of their church connections and financial interests, King's
grandfather and, later, his father were members of the ruling elite of
Atlanta's Negro community which was considered by some the dis-
tilled essence of what E. Franklin Frazier called the Black Puritan

class. The Negro-owned and Negro-operated businesses of Auburn Avenue and the French Normandy mansions and neat Georgians of the affluent Negro leadership class confirmed the basic postulates of the group: that a Negro could "make it," if he studied hard, worked hard, and stayed out of trouble. And what was trouble? Trouble was a palpable presence called the white man.

A shadow of the plantation and of slavery, a Black Puritan paradise, a presence called trouble, and a tradition of hard work, thrift, service, responsibility, and sacrifice: from this soil came Martin Luther King, Jr. As a child, King was a healthy, vital, fun-loving male with many playmates, most of whom he dominated by will power and an instinctive gift of words. The King backyard, large and spacious, and the vacant lot beyond were something of a neighborhood gathering point. Here, in summer and winter, young King played sandlot baseball and football and measured himself in trials of strength with his peers. The future advocate of nonviolence proved so adept at these trials of strength that his playmates would say later that his playing was not always distinguishable from fighting. "You took a chance," one of them recalled later, "in getting hurt even when you were playing football or basketball for fun against him."

Almost from the beginning, however, young Martin made words and symbols central to his orientation to life. Watching his father and other ministers dominate audiences with artfully chosen words, the young boy tingled with excitement; and the urge to speak, to express himself, to turn and twist and lift audiences, seized him and never afterwards left him. To form words into sentences, to fling them out on the waves of air in a crescendo of sound, to watch people weep, shout, respond: this fascinated young Martin. His mother has said that she cannot recall a time when he was not fascinated by the sound and power of words. "You just wait and see," he told his mother at the age of six, "I'm going to get me some big words." The idea of using words as weapons of defense and offense was thus early implanted and seems to have grown in King as naturally as a flower. In time, this idea would become a central component of his life style. Years later, he would tell his friend and biographer, Lawrence D. Reddick, that his "greatest talent, strongest tradition, and most constant interest" was not action but "the eloquent statement of ideas." King's brief career as a soprano soloist was an extension of his original projection of himself toward symbol-oriented possibilities. At the age of four or five, the future preacher attracted a great deal of attention at church conventions with rhythmically persuasive renditions of the gospel song, "I Want To Be More Like Jesus."

King and his older sister, Christine, and his younger brother, Alfred Daniel, were raised in comfortable, middle-class circumstances. King was born on the lip of the Great Depression and grew up in a community where almost 65 per cent of the Negro population was on public relief, but these currents never touched the even tenor of his life. There was always meat on the King table, and bread and butter. "We've never lived in a rented house," the elder King has said, "and never *ridden* too long in a car on which payment was due."

It was a secure world. King's childhood, unlike the childhood of millions of other American Negroes, was marked by order, balance, and restraint: Sunday School, church, and BYPU on Sunday, playtime in or near the house on weekdays, an afternoon job throwing papers (not necessarily for money but for *discipline* and training), early to bed, early to rise. Days began and ended in the King home with family prayers, and King and his brother and sister were required to learn Bible verses for recitation at evening meals.

The suggestion of order and balance was accentuated by the contrasting personalities of the parents. The father was volatile, emotional, trigger-tempered; the mother was calm, cool, slow to anger, deliberate in speech and action. Their oldest son seems to be an exquisite cross between these two temperaments. Although placid qualities seem to be dominant in his personality structure, there are latent seeds of his father's fire. King has said, in an exceptionally acute self-analysis, that he is an "ambivert—half introvert and half extrovert." The overemphasis on the placidity of his temperament has served to obfuscate a deeper and more ambivalent strain; and the tension between these two strains, between the extrovert and the introvert, is probably a root element in the oak of his greatness. The fact, as L. D. Reddick pointed out, that King "seems to have attempted suicide" twice before his thirteenth birthday should warn us that we are dealing with a man of considerable complexity. The first incident occurred after his beloved grandmother, Jennie Williams, was accidentally knocked unconscious. King, thinking she was dead, ran upstairs and leaped from a second-story window. For a moment, it seemed that he had killed himself. He lay motionless, oblivious to the screams of relatives. Then, as though nothing had happened, he got up and walked away. In 1941, on the death of the grandmother, King again leaped from the second-story window and, again, he survived.

Childhood is a time of terrors and vague fears for all children. For a Negro child, who must come to terms not only with himself but with the uneasy knowledge that the world knows something about him and his past, something considered shameful and delimiting, childhood is a period filled with monstrous shapes and shadows. King's childhood does not seem to have differed significantly from the usual pattern. His world, it is true, was more secure than the worlds of most Negroes, but the same shadow that menaced other Negroes lay athwart the sun of his world. Like all Negro children, Martin felt the shadow before he saw it. There were places he could not go. There were things he could not do. There were instruments, objects, people, he had to avoid. Out there in the world was something monstrous and menacing, more terrible perhaps because no one could reduce it to words a little boy could understand. Because of his privileged position in a privileged family, the shadow was not an omnipresent reality. But it was out there, on the periphery of vision, and one day the shadow fell.

Among King's closest childhood friends were the two children of the neighborhood grocer. "None of us," King has recalled, "seriously thought anything about those white boys being different, and we played with them all the time until we were ready for school. Well, they went to the white school and I went to another, and I still didn't think much about it at first. But suddenly when I would run across the street after school to compare notes, their mother would tell them that they could not play anymore. She said they were white and I was colored. At first, she just made excuses, but finally she told me. I think I cried, but anyway I rushed home and asked mother about it."

The mother brushed away the tears and sat down, undoubtedly with a sigh, to tell her son about the blacks and whites of American life. Digging deep into history, searching for the right words, or, rather, for words a six-year-old could understand, she recounted the centuries of slavery and segregation and explained the fears and foibles of man. Then she said: "Don't let this thing impress you. Don't let it make you feel you are not as good as white people. You are as good as anyone else, and don't you forget it."

So there it was, out in the open, big and blooming and white. Young Martin looked at the thing, impressed despite himself. So he was colored. But what, precisely, did that mean? Young Martin turned around within himself and looked at himself and his world.

A second encounter, two years later, when he was eight, deepened his anxiety. He went one day to downtown Five Points with his father

to buy a pair of shoes. Father and son took seats in the front of the
store. A white clerk approached and said:

"I'll be happy to wait on you if you'll just move back there to those
seats in the rear."

"Nothing wrong with these seats," the elder King harrumphed.

"Sorry," said the clerk, "but you'll *have* to go back there."

"We'll either buy shoes sitting here," the father shot back, flaring
up, "or we won't buy any shoes at all." King took his son by the hand
and stomped from the store, fuming. Looking back on this encounter,
later, the son said: "It was probably the first time I had seen Daddy
so furious, and I guess I was hurt for the first time too. Daddy has always been an emotional man, and I can remember him muttering: 'I
don't care how long I have to live with this system, I am never going
to accept it. I'll oppose it until the day I die.' "

What made this incident so painful, however, to both father and
son, was that *he had* to accept not only that but a great deal more.
This fact forced thought on young King, intensifying his awareness.
The established order which had seemed so safe and secure turned out
on inspection to conceal a horrible disorder. A yawning abyss opened
beneath his feet. He had to rethink his relation to himself and to the
world. Who was he? And what? The education of Martin Luther King,
Jr., began.

The seasons turned slowly for the growing boy, rounding the curve
of the Depression and heading into the crisis of World War II. King
entered the public schools in 1935, transferred later to the private labo-
ratory school at Atlanta University and then entered Booker T. Washington High School. At school, King was a good—almost model—student, deferential to his elders, considerate of his peers. Somewhat
precocious and hard-working, King skipped the ninth grade at Booker
T. Washington and entered the sophomore class in the fall of 1942.

By that time, the family fortunes had improved tremendously and
King's father, carrying out his childhood vow, bought a yellow-brick
house on Boulevard Street in a more substantial neighborhood;
the elder King had become a major force in the Negro community. As
a powerful pastor with substantial business interests, he served on the
board of the Negro-owned bank and on the governing boards of institutions like Atlanta University, Morehouse, and the National Baptist

Convention. King's father was also a power in the local NAACP branch and the Atlanta Negro Voters League. Because of his uncompromising stands as a racial leader, the elder King often received threatening telephone calls and abusive letters from the Ku Klux Klan.

It was in this climate that Martin Luther King, Jr., spent his formative years. In school and out of school, young Martin assimilated the major facts of his environment. He learned that he was a male and what that meant, that he was a Negro male and what that meant, that he was the son of an important man and what that meant, and that he was expected to succeed and become important and useful himself.

Like most young boys, young Martin was two boys: the mild-mannered student who accommodated himself to the foibles of his elders and the smooth-talking teenager who danced on every number, who smoked a first cigarette behind a fence, and who changed girls almost as often as he changed the tweed suits he adored. The confusion of these two boys seems to lie at the root of the myth-encrusted theory that King was born nonviolent. It is not necessary really to seek in this period for the provenance of King's ideas on nonviolence. Gandhis are not born; they invent themselves. What we must seek in this soil is not the embryonic Gandhi but the emerging pattern that made Gandhism attractive to King and the inner mechanisms that inclined him toward a radical rejection of the protest perspective of the leadership class into which he was born.

The record, which is contradictory, seems to indicate that King was an even-tempered youth who avoided, whenever possible, non-middle-class fights, i.e., fights with sticks and stones and knives. It is said that King, when walloped by the neighborhood bully, turned the other cheek; and that he bit his lips and remained silent when a white woman slapped him. But the same record, particularly the reminiscences of his peers as distinguished from the reminiscences of adults, who are notoriously unreliable as character witnesses for youth, clearly indicates that King was a master at the acceptable trials of strength of his group.

In King's peer group, vital, non-negotiable decisions were decided by physical combat. The aggrieved or the provoking party was always free to hurl the ritual challenge, "Let's go to the grass," an invitation to a trial by middle-class combat. Most members of King's childhood circle say it was King who invented this phrase. At any rate, they all agree that King was not slow in hurling or accepting such challenges.

Morehouse College, which played important
role in King's development, is all-men's
institution which has molded large number
of Negro leaders, ministers, educators. King's
grandfather and father also attended Morehouse.

The Rev. Benjamin E. Mays, major influence in King's life, is pictured in his office at Morehouse College Morehouse president is eloquent preacher and a national leader. He played key role in King's decision to enter ministry. Picture (background) is of John Hope, first Negro president of Morehouse.

Of additional interest here is the fact that King seems to have had few-
er fights than usual because of his increasing success in manipulating
his environment via symbols. His brother, A. D. King, has said, significantly: "He didn't fight much. He usually was able to talk any situation to a conclusion."

King was not yet a Gandhian, but there were seeds in his personality
structure that pointed in that direction. Basically, there are only two
life approaches to power: resistance or submission. But King seems to
have adopted quite early a psychological posture that bridged the two.
Nothing indicates this more clearly than his responses to his father,
who fulfilled, in an affectionate and fiercely protective way, St. Paul's
idea of the head of a family. By all accounts, King and his brother and
sister responded to their father's fiats in different ways. Christine, it is
said, usually submitted, and A. D. revolted. And young Martin? He
neither revolted nor submitted. He heard his father out, patiently and
respectfully, and then did what he wanted to do. Long before King
heard of Gandhi or India, he had mastered the technique of resisting
by apparent submission. This was, in part, a projection of his personal
life style. But it reflected, too, the social styles of the Negro people
who survived in America by resisting while apparently submitting.

One other factor in King's personality requires emphasis. There was
in him, even as a youth, a quiet but nonetheless tenacious stubborn-
ness. "He was," his father said, "the most peculiar child whenever you
whipped him. He'd stand there, and the tears would run down and he'd
never cry. His grandmother couldn't stand to see it." Flowing with and
out of this was a will of steel. Behind the calm exterior was an edge of
fire. All who knew him then comment on that fact. He could not be
pushed too far. "I remember once," A. D. King said, "that I was giving our sister Christine . . . a hard time, and he told me to cut it out. I
kept on with whatever I was doing, and M. L. suddenly reached over
and picked up the telephone. I thought he was going to call Daddy or
Mother, wherever they were, but he didn't. He conked me over the
head with that phone and almost knocked my brains out."

Beneath the placid surface of young King's life other currents moved.
He dissented apparently from crucial postulates of the Black Puritan
world view. Black Puritans, then and now, worshipped success and
held themselves aloof from the Negro masses. But King had—and has
—deep sympathies for the masses and a barely concealed contempt
for the standards of success of his class. Even more astonishing, King

was repelled by the Negro religious tradition which was a major agglutinative factor in Negro life but which was scarcely more relevant to the real problems of the Negro masses than the white Christian church. King's father wanted him to be a minister, but King decided quite early that he was *not* going to be a minister. It seemed to him then that religion could not be intellectually respectable and socially relevant. He decided, therefore, to become a doctor. It would appear, however, that Alfred Adler's dictum, "Man *knows* more than he understands," applies to the King of this period. For although King *said* he wanted to study medicine, he continued to sharpen the non-medical skills, particularly oratory, that would later bring him fame. During his last year in high school, he reached what he considered the summit of his youthful achievements, winning an Elks oratorical contest. The subject of his discourse, he said, was "something about the Negro and the Constitution."

What was more important than the deepening of King's interest in oratory was the steady unfolding of the theme that was to dominate and shape his life. From his early teens onward, he was increasingly sensitive to the daily pinpricks and insults Negroes suffered in the South. One incident of these years stands out as foretaste and prophecy. Returning from an oratorical contest in Valdosta, Georgia, King and his fellow students took the first bus seats they could find. The bus driver ordered them to move, but they refused until their Negro teacher suggested that it would be best. Enraged by this revolt against the system, the driver ranted and raved, calling King and his fellow students "black sons of bitches." The Negro students endured this abuse in silence, if not in love. Looking back, later, King said: "It was a night I'll never forget. I don't think I have ever been so deeply angry in my life."

A trip to the North in the summer of 1944 intensified King's despair. In Hartford, Connecticut, and other Northern cities, he noted with pleasure the absence of Jim Crow signs. More importantly, he did not detect in the air the miasma of fear and anxiety that lay like a scourge over the segregated South. Returning to the South after this experience was "a bitter pill." When, on the return trip, he was seated behind a curtain in a dining car, he said he felt "as if the curtain had been dropped on my selfhood." As a result of these experiences and others of similar weight and meaning, King came "perilously close" to hating white people. Of greater immediate consequence was his decision to become a lawyer. "I was at that point," he said, "where I was deeply interested in political matters and social ills. I could envision myself playing a part in breaking down the legal barriers to Negro rights."

It was a new King who returned to Atlanta in 1944. He seemed older and more mature. His mother remarked on that fact, saying he "seemed changed." King had always been a deliberate, methodical type who exfoliated slowly, sending deep roots into the ground. Now, at last, he seemed sure of himself and what he wanted to do with his life. To prepare himself for his future role as a legal champion of the Negro people, he began to practice his speeches in front of a mirror.

The year 1944, at the beginning of which Martin Luther King, Jr. turned fifteen, marked a new phase in his development. He had already skipped the ninth grade at Booker T. Washington High School. Now, by taking and passing a college entrance examination, he also skipped the twelfth grade, completing his high school work at the age of fifteen. In September, he followed a family tradition by entering Morehouse College. Morehouse was an all-men's school, famous for molding leading members of the Negro leadership group. At Morehouse, the pursuit of excellence in the classroom was supplemented by daily chapel periods and a vigorous and exceptionally free campus life. Two things were drilled into Morehouse men from their first day on the campus to their last: 1) that they were Morehouse men and 2) that they were expected to succeed in life. What impressed young King, above all, was the sense of freedom on the Morehouse campus. "There was a freer atmosphere at Morehouse," he has said, "and it was there that I had my first frank discussion on race. The professors were not caught up in the clutches of state funds and could teach what they wanted with academic freedom. They encouraged us in a positive quest for a salvation to racial ills and *for the first time in my life, I realized that nobody there was afraid.*" [Emphasis supplied.]

It was a revelation, this, and the revelation, fleshed out in the lives of bold and intellectually vigorous teachers, unlocked new possibilities in King's mind. Within a short time, he was a familiar figure on the Morehouse campus, which occupies a hill in west Atlanta. He was, at that time, a rather short, plump-faced youth, healthy, confident, questing. Benjamin E. Mays, the college president, remembers him then as an unusually serious and sensitive young man. Mays spoke usually at Tuesday morning chapel sessions. After chapel, King would often question Mays about the subject of the day. Mays said later: "I perceived immediately that this boy was mature beyond his years; that he spoke as a man who should have had ten more years' experience than was possible. He had a balance and maturity then that were far beyond his years and a grasp of life and its problems that exceeded even that."

As a sociology major, King made an excellent classroom record. He did not, however, make a large impact on campus life. He sang in the glee club but joined only a few organizations, none of which elected him to high office. He was also active as an orator, winning a prize in the annual college oratorical contest.

During King's undergraduate days, the Morehouse campus was alive with political and social ferment. On one occasion, a campus strike and boycott of the dining room raised tensions to a record high. But, curiously, the future rebel held himself aloof from these radical currents. King's detachment from the vital currents of campus life can be explained by two facts: 1) he was a city student who lived off campus; and 2) he was deeply divided within himself, searching for something he could not name. Although he had outwardly committed himself to law, he was still "wrestling inside with the problem of a vocation." Deep down inside, he wanted to be a minister, but he was still repelled by the "emotionalism," the hand-clapping, "amen-ing," and shouting of the Negro church. Moreover, he believed that there was an oversupply of "unintellectual" and "untrained ministers" in the Negro church.

Morehouse widened King's understanding of himself and of the service he could perform in the world. The college was served at that juncture by a number of outstanding ministers, including Dr. Mays, the president, and Dr. George D. Kelsey, director of the department of religion. Both Mays and Kelsey were seminary-trained ministers, and their sermons, socially relevant and intellectually stimulating, changed King's mind about the ministry. In Mays and Kelsey, he saw the ideal of what he wanted "a real minister to be." Finally, in his junior year, he decided to give himself to the ministry. He immediately informed his mother, who told him—as he knew she would—to tell his father. King, with no little trepidation, approached his father, who was pleased though he did not, at first, admit it. The elder King said gravely that he wanted to be "reassured." To this end, a trial sermon was arranged. Thinking back on it later, the father said: "He was just seventeen and he started giving the sermon—I don't remember the subject—in the first unit of the church and the crowds kept coming, and we had to move to the main auditorium." Martin Luther King, Sr., was too well bred to vent his satisfaction before his son. But he went home that night and got down on his knees and thanked God. In 1947, the son was ordained and named assistant pastor of his father's church.

Sure of himself now and of his mission, the Rev. Martin Luther King, Jr., waded out into the depths as a servant of God. It was during this period that he began to reach out in a tentative, inchoate way to the Negro masses. Between school sessions at Morehouse, he sought jobs that would expose him to the plight of the masses. As the son of a prominent Negro leader, he could have worked in any one of several Negro-owned businesses. But he chose instead to work as a laborer, toiling one summer at the Railway Express Company, unloading trains and trucks, and another summer at the Southern Spring Bed Mattress Company as a stockroom helper. Both jobs were laborious and backbreaking, but King said he wanted to work with the masses to "learn their plight and to feel their feelings." These episodes, though slight, were full of meaning. A seed was planted in King during these summers that grew with the passing years. He observed with interest during these interludes that Negro males were paid markedly less than white males performing the same jobs. He had been told in Professor Walter Chivers' sociology classes that money was the root not only of evil but also of race. But now he saw the theory in action and he would never forget it.

Another milestone in King's development was an incidental by-product of his membership in the city's integrated Intercollegiate Council. Mingling with whites for the first time on a basis of substantial equality, King developed a more complex view of race. "The whole-some relations we had in this group," he said later, "convinced me that we have many white persons as allies, particularly among the younger generation. I had been ready to resent the whole white race, but as I got to see more white people my resentment was softened and a spirit of cooperation took its place."

During this same period of great growth and discovery, King seems to have come to a deeper understanding of his mission in life. An arti-cle which he wrote for the college newspaper, the *Maroon Tiger*, in 1948 on "The Purpose of Education" foreshadowed his future useful-ness. King began by noting that "most" of his fellow students seemed to think that "education should equip them with the proper instrument of exploitation so that they can forever trample over the masses." It seemed to him that education should furnish men with "noble ends rather than means to an end." King, then nineteen, wrote:

> At this point, I often wonder whether or not education is fulfilling its purpose. A great majority of the so-called educated people do not think logically and scientifically. Even the press, the classroom, the platform, and the pulpit in many instances do not give us objective and unbiased truths. To save man from the morass of propaganda, in my opinion, is one of the chief aims of education. Education must enable one to sift and weigh evidence, to discern the true from the false, the real from the unreal, and the facts from fiction.
>
> The function of education, therefore, is to teach one to think intensively and to think critically. But education which stops with efficiency may prove the greatest menace to society. The most dangerous criminal may be the man gifted with reason, but with no morals.
>
> The late Eugene Talmadge, in my opinion, possessed one of the better minds of Georgia, or even America. Moreover, he wore the Phi Beta Kappa key. By all measuring rods, Mr. Talmadge could think critically and intensively; yet he contends that I am an inferior being. . . .
>
> We must remember that intelligence is not enough. Intelligence plus character—that is the goal of true education. The complete education gives one not only power of concentration, but worthy objectives upon which to concentrate. The broad education will, therefore, transmit to one not only the accumulated knowledge of the race but also the accumulated experience of social living.

"Intelligence plus character" and a concern for the masses: these words from the pen of young Martin describe rather accurately the height to which he had come in nineteen short years. There remained only the quest for "noble ends" "upon which to concentrate" and the invention of the proper instruments of liberation. In June, 1948, a month and a year heavy with the promise of new grass, Martin Luther King, Jr., was graduated from Morehouse College with a bachelor of arts degree. He was nineteen years of age. The road to the high mountain of the world lay open before him, and the sun was in his face.

Seed

As MARTIN LUTHER KING, JR., moved, in the fall of 1948, from Atlanta, Georgia, to Crozer Theological Seminary in Chester, Pennsylvania, he was uneasily aware of a change in the spirit of the world. The root-shaking dislocations of World War II, the central event of his formative years, had unleashed forces that were destroying the old racial equilibrium. All over the world now, in India, in Africa, in America, brown, black, and yellow men were pushing their heads above the water; and Europeans, feeling themselves watched, weighed, *judged*, were retreating in perplexity and anxiety.

King, coming to maturity in this era of stress and change, sensed—dimly at first and then with ever-increasing clarity—the implications of this worldwide upheaval. While still an undergraduate at Morehouse College he had noted, with approval, the new spirit of assertiveness in the Negro ghetto. He had been too young in 1942 to comprehend Asa Philip Randolph's attempt to form a national civil disobedience movement based on Gandhian tactics. But Randolph's threat, in 1947, to

lead a civil disobedience movement in protest against a segregated
army, had stirred not only King but thousands of young Negro college
students. Now, as King unpacked his bags in the Crozer dormitory,
the land was ablaze with controversy over the Progressive party and
Harry Truman's uphill fight for a "strong" civil rights bill. King
watched, nourished, as the Negro ethos expanded. It was a sign, this,
a sign of what King would later call the Zeitgeist stirring in the womb
of time. In the hour when the Negro spirit changed from patient
resignation to outreaching expectancy, King's destiny began to take
shape. Though King did not know it, the Zeitgeist was stalking him
and preparing him for a later and more definitive engagement with a
crumbling and outdated world view.

But none of this was apparent to King in September, 1948. What
deeply engaged his attention at that moment were the facts, first, that
he was away from home for the first time in his life; and, second, that
he was on trial. As one of six Negro students in a student body of some
one hundred, King was competing for the first time with white Americans. He had been taught, at home and at Morehouse, that he was as
good as the next man. But it is impossible to grasp reality without performing an operation on it. Determined to prove self and race, feeling
himself watched and judged, feeling, moreover, that he was responsible
not only for himself but for all Negroes, King threw himself into
his studies with a vengeance. He admitted later that he tended, at first,
to overreact, anticipating the palpable and hostile consciousness of the
white Other. He told William Peters of Redbook magazine: "I was
well aware of the typical white stereotype of the Negro, that he is always late, that he's loud and always laughing, that he's dirty and messy,
and for a while I was terribly conscious of trying to avoid identification
with it. If I were a minute late to class, I was almost morbidly conscious of it and sure that everyone else noticed it. Rather than be
thought of as always laughing, I'm afraid I was grimly serious for a
time. I had a tendency to overdress, to keep my room spotless, my
shoes perfectly shined and my clothes immaculately pressed."

Grim, ferociously scrubbed and forbiddingly serious, King bested his
white classmates in the usual seminary fare of Bible criticism, church
history, church administration, and practice preaching. With increasing success came increasing confidence. Long before the end of the
three-year Crozer course, King knew beyond a shadow of doubt that a
brain is a brain and that the package, as Howard Thurman has said,
doesn't matter.

King maintained excellent relations with his white classmates,
developing some friendships that extended beyond the seminary. There

were, however, the usual stresses and strains that develop among youths raised in segregated communities. At Crozer, as in other institutions, students relieved the day-by-day tension with pranks and hijinks. A favorite stratagem, beloved by students since the construction of the first college dormitory, was the "room raid," the disarrangement in jest of a classmate's room, the overturning of chairs, beds, and personal effects. From time to time, most of the Crozer students, King included, were either perpetrators or victims of this prank, which was received good-naturedly by most. On one occasion, however, a white student from North Carolina took violent exception to the disarrangement of his room. Worse, he focused his fire on King, brandishing a pistol and threatening to end his Negro classmate's life. King, who had not been involved in *that* raid, remained calm, outwardly at any rate. He denied the accusations and suggested that the white student was unduly excited. By this time, the altercation had attracted a large group of students, who calmed the North Carolinian and forced him to put away the gun. The incident, which created a furore on the campus, died down after the white student apologized publicly and confessed his error. By graduation time, King and the North Carolinian were fast friends.

Always sociable, despite his fondness for contemplation, young Martin used his spare time at Crozer to improve his knowledge of the world. He attended parties in Philadelphia and nearby suburbs and was a regular spectator at the Penn Relays. He was also a frequent guest at the home of J. Pius Barbour, a Morehouse and Crozer graduate whose home was near the seminary.

King's racial philosophy at this juncture was orthodox. He leaned at that time and for several years thereafter toward the NAACP legal approach. This is confirmed by his response to one of several racial incidents that marred this phase of his life. When King and a fellow classmate and two young ladies were refused service at a restaurant near Camden, New Jersey, they refused at first to yield their seats. The manager, enraged, ran outside, fired his pistol into the air and shouted: "I'll kill for less." King and his friends then decided that it would be best to leave. But they returned a few minutes later with a policeman. The manager was arrested and the King party secured statements from several customers. They later filed suit, through the Camden NAACP branch, charging violation of the New Jersey civil rights law. However, at this point, the witnesses backed down and the case spluttered to an inconclusive end.

King was a perfect student at Crozer, maintaining an A average for the three-year course. He also found time to take supplemental courses

in philosophy at the University of Pennsylvania. Although this schedule consumed most of his working hours, King was far from satisfied.
Finding no answers, apparently, in his classrooms to the burning questions that were troubling his mind, he began to read ravenously, devouring book after book in "a serious intellectual quest for a method
to eliminate social evil."

Of all the authors he read in this period (Reinhold Niebuhr, Marx,
Sartre, Jaspers, Heidegger), two impressed him most. The first was
Hegel, whose analysis of the dialectical process and of progress and
growth through pain became central elements in his emerging personal
philosophy. King was impressed, too, by Hegel's theory that "World-
historical individuals" were the agents by which "the will of the World
Spirit" is carried out. It is likely that the troubled, questing student
also read and remembered the following Hegelian quote which would
later apply, almost word for word, to him:

> They may all be called Heroes, in as much as they have derived
> their purposes and their vocation, not from the calm regular course
> of things, sanctioned by the existing order; but from a concealed
> fount, from that inner Spirit, still hidden beneath the surface, which
> impinges on the outer world as on a shell and bursts into pieces.
> (Such were Alexander, Caesar, Napoleon.) They were practical,
> political men. But at the same time they were thinking men, who
> had an insight into the requirements of the time—what was ripe for
> development. This was the very truth for their age, for their world
> . . . . It was theirs to know this nascent principle, the necessary, di-
> rectly sequent step in progress, which their world was to take; to make
> this their aim, and to expend their energy in promoting it. World-
> historical men—the Heroes of an epoch—must therefore be recog-
> nized as its clear-sighted ones: *their* deeds, *their* words are the best
> of their time.

Hegel's theory, of course was—and is—amoral. It could be used by
either a Gandhi or a Hitler. What was necessary was an informing insight leading to "noble ends." King found a glimmer of that light in
the works and words of a second man, Walter Rauschenbusch, the articulate exponent of the social gospel. In 1950, during his senior year at
Crozer, King came across a copy of Rauschenbusch's *Christianity and*

the Social Crisis, a book which he said, "left an indelible imprint on my thinking." Although King did not agree with the whole of Rauschenbusch's philosophy, he was "fascinated" by the great preacher's application of the social principles of Jesus to the problems of the modern world. Thereafter, the main thrust of the "social gospel"—the idea that the church should take a direct, active role in the struggle for social justice—became a pivotal element in King's personal philosophy.

That same year, 1950, King was exposed to nonviolence as a technique and Gandhi as a prophet. There was, first of all, a campus lecture by A. J. Muste, a Christian rebel who championed a nonviolent approach as the leading light of the Fellowship of Reconciliation, a predominantly-white pacifist group. King was not overly impressed by the Muste lecture. Though he loathed war, he believed then that the "turn-the-other-cheek and the love-your-enemies philosophy" was only valid in conflicts between individuals and not in bone-deep disagreements between racial groups and nations.

Another lecture, this one by Mordecai Johnson, then president of Howard University, thrust further thought upon him. Johnson, a graduate of Morehouse and a powerful Baptist preacher, had returned from a 1950 visit to India with a deep conviction that Gandhi's tactics were applicable to the race struggle in America. After his return, he delivered several evangelical sermons on nonviolence and the redemptive power of love and unmerited suffering. When, on a Sunday afternoon in 1950, he spoke at the Fellowship House of Philadelphia, King was in the audience. Stirred not only by Johnson's message but also by Johnson's fervor, King went out immediately and bought, he said, a "half-dozen books on Gandhi's life and works." As an educated man, King had a certain familiarity with Gandhi's heroic efforts to free India from British rule. Gandhi's campaign, which began long before King was born, covered a thirty-year span. During this period Gandhi employed a variety of techniques, fasts, general strikes, boycotts, mass marches, and massive civil disobedience. The key to his vision of battle, however, was nonresistance or *Satyagraha* which has been translated as soul force, the power of truth. *Satyagraha,* Gandhi wrote, "is the vindication of truth not by infliction of suffering on the opponent but on one's self." Throughout the long contest with Britain, Gandhi urged his followers to forswear violence and to work for ultimate reconciliation with their opponents by returning good for evil and by openly breaking unjust laws and willingly paying the penalty. "Rivers of blood," he said in a quote King would later repeat, almost word for word, "may have to flow before we gain our freedom, but it must be our blood."

Suffering and self-sacrifice were at the heart of Gandhi's philosophy. "The government of the day," he said, "has passed a law which is applicable to me. I do not like it. If by using violence I force the government to repeal the law, I am employing what may be called body-force. If I do not obey the law and accept the penalty for the breach, I use soul-force. It involves sacrifice of self. . . ."

Reading these words and others of similar tone and texture in 1950, King, then twenty-one and at a crucial turning point in his own development, was impressed despite himself. Yet he held back, seeking further clarification in the life and thoughts of Gandhi. The Gandhian philosophy, which King considered briefly at this juncture, was far from alien. Gandhi himself was deeply influenced by Henry David Thoreau, who had, in turn, been influenced by the *Bhagavad-Gita* and other sacred texts of the East. By an extraordinary turn of fate, King would later rekindle on American soil a doctrine that had crossed and recrossed the seas in a remarkable cross-pollenation of ideas.

Influenced by the Indian world view *and* the struggle for freedom of King's forebears, Thoreau decided in the mid-nineteenth century that "the only obligation which I have the right to assume is to do at any time what I think right." Like Gandhi, Thoreau believed that the power of resistance on the part of a minority was enormous, given a fixed will to win at that particular point and a willingness to pay the price. "I know this well," he wrote, "that if one thousand, if one hundred, if ten men whom I could name—if ten *honest* men only— ay, if one *HONEST* man, in this state of Massachusetts, *ceasing to hold slaves*, were actually to withdraw from this co-partnership [with the government] and be locked up in the county jail therefor, it would be the abolition of slavery in America. . . ." Thoreau practiced what he preached. He was jailed once for refusing to pay his taxes. When his distinguished friend, Ralph Waldo Emerson, approached and asked, "Thoreau, why are you in jail?" Thoreau replied, "Emerson, why are you out of jail?"

That idea, the idea that jail is the place for good men when social evil threatens the soul and spirit of man, permeated Thoreau's *Essay on Civil Disobedience*, which Gandhi read for the first time in a South African jail. Fusing his own insights with Thoreau's ideas and the admonitions of Jesus ("resist not evil"), Gandhi fashioned a philosophy of "war without violence" that brought the British Empire to bay. (Gandhi was helped enormously, however, by the currents released by mankind's most violent act, World War II.)

Martin Luther King, Jr. found all this extremely enlightening and spiritually exalting. But he was not sure it would work in America. Gandhi led a majority against a minority. Moreover, the antagonisms between the British and Indians were relatively superficial when compared with the swirling pits of emotion beneath the Negro-white situation. Though impressed by Gandhi, King was far from converted. He filed the idea in his mind with others collected during the period.

Stimulated not only by his classroom work but also by his extramural forays into the germinal insights of Hegel, Gandhi, and Rauschenbusch, King was graduated, in June, 1951, from Crozer Theological Seminary. He left Crozer with an enviable record. He won the Plafker Award as the most outstanding student, was president of the senior class, and received the J. Lewis Crozer fellowship of $1200 for graduate study at a university of his choice.

With new confidence in himself and his possibilities, King enrolled in Boston University as a graduate student in philosophy. He traveled to Boston the next fall in a green Chevrolet, a graduation present from his parents. After the first semester, King and an old friend from Morehouse, Philip Lenud, rented a suite of rooms at 397 Massachusetts Avenue. The suite consisted of two bedrooms, a kitchen, bath, and a large living room. Before long, Lenud, a divinity student at Tufts College, and King were serving as catalysts for the Negro students at Boston area colleges. Their friends, however, were not confined to any one race or creed. Students of varying backgrounds and beliefs thronged the Massachusetts Avenue apartment where hot coffee and stimulating ideas were always available. This intellectual ferment was structured with the organization, by King and Lenud, of the Philosophical Club, a group of Negro graduate students who held weekly meetings at the King-Lenud apartment.

King had remained, up to this point, something of a spectator of life. Cool, detached, sure of his goal, which he was approaching according to a timetable he had drawn up, King had avoided giving hostages to the future. He had, it is true, what has been called "an understanding" with a childhood sweetheart, but he had shown no indications of what his father called "settling down." This disturbed the elder King no end, for he believed that no good could come to a handsome, intelligent young man, alone in a big city.

From adolescence on, King had been unusually successful in winning girl friends and avoiding entangling alliances. During his Crozer career, he had been pursued, unsuccessfully, by several young women, including a wealthy young white student. According to a "close friend," interviewed by Ted Poston of the *New York Post*, King "steeled" himself against the white student, although she "was a perfect lady." He reportedly told his friend: "She liked me and I found myself liking her. But finally I had to tell her resolutely that my plans for the future did not include marriage to a white woman." The truth of the matter seems to be that King's "plans for the future" did not include marriage to anyone at that juncture. But now, quite unexpectedly, he fell in love. Coretta Scott, the pretty, long-haired soprano Martin Luther King, Jr., married, has said that she had an eerie feeling when she met King that it had been somehow preordained and that she and Martin had been approaching each other on separate roads of fate.

One of the roads began far to the South in Heiberger, Alabama, where Coretta Scott was born. Like King, Coretta was the second of three children. Unlike King, she was a child of struggle. She was born on April 27, 1927, to Obadiah (Obie) and Bernie McMurry Scott. The Scotts had deep roots in the soil of Perry County where their forebears had owned land since the Civil War. By the late fifties, Coretta's father owned a store, several trucks, a farm, and considerable estate. But the family barely scraped through the trying days of the Depression. In this period, Coretta recalled, her father had a great deal of trouble with local whites. "Whites," she said, "resented him. He was in direct competition with them, and for a period of several years, he would come home talking about the threats he got. Some even stopped him in the middle of the road and pulled out their guns." He used to say, "If you look a white man in the eyes, he won't harm you." This theory which proved apt to Obie Scott's purposes, caused the children considerable concern. "We were quite young then," Coretta Scott King has said, "and we were afraid something would happen to him. He would go out at night to work, and we never knew whether he would be coming back or not."

In this atmosphere, in a county where the seven thousand ruling whites were always conscious of the human aspirations of the twenty thousand subject blacks, Coretta Scott grew into an awareness of herself as a human being, a female, and a Negro. Analyzing this situation many years later in an article published by *Opportunity* magazine while she was a student at Antioch College, Coretta said: "The struggles of my family were not unique . . . but typical of the larger Southern pattern, and perhaps an intensification of a still larger pattern of living into which people like me were forced in our American society." But this was the fruit of dawning maturity. As a child, Coretta felt the problem with part of her mind while reaching out with the other part to life.

The future wife of the world's leading advocate of passive resistance was, as a child, a tomboy and a fighter who delighted in flailing her brother and other playmates with hoes, sticks, rocks, and anything else that came to hand. "I have always had a temper," she would say later. "Mother said I was the meanest girl. I used to fight all the time."

From time to time, as a child, Coretta supplemented the family's Depression income by hiring herself out to hoe and to pick cotton. But she, like young Martin, came early to books, which she believed were means to her two ends: 1) "the burning desire to be treated as an equal" and 2) the equally compelling desire "to do something for humanity."

At the Crossroads School, a small frame building, Coretta breezed through the first six grades as the top student in her classes. She then entered Lincoln School in nearby Marion. Lincoln School, a private missionary institution with Negro and white teachers, opened up a whole new world to the growing girl. Here, she became interested in music; and from here, in 1945, she went with the aid of a race relations scholarship to Antioch College in Yellow Springs, Ohio. Coretta's sister had preceded her by two years, becoming, in 1943, the first Negro full-time student to live on campus.

At Dexter Avenue Baptist Church in downtown Montgomery, King receives parishioners at end of morning services. He became international figure while serving as pastor of historic church which occupies central role in life of Montgomery Negro community. He served as pastor of church from September 1, 1954, to January 31, 1960.

After garden ceremony at home of bride's parents
in Heiberger, Alabama, Martin Luther King, Jr.,
then twenty-four, and Coretta Scott King pose
for traditional wedding picture.

Antioch at the time was well known for its work-study program which provided classroom and work experiences for students. Under this plan, which was designed to broaden students by exposing them to life as well as books, students spent one-half of their college career in the classroom and the remaining time working on campus or in far-away cities. During the six years Coretta spent in this extended program, she worked as a waitress on campus, as a librarian in New York City, and as a counsellor at Karamu House in Cleveland. On campus, she majored in elementary education. Although her most consuming interest was music, she planned at that time to teach school. On November 9, 1948, the same fall Martin Luther King entered Crozer, she made her debut as a soprano soloist at the Second Baptist Church in Springfield, Ohio.

From a psychological standpoint, there is only a small difference between being excluded from a white institution and being accepted by a white institution as a "token" Negro. After two years of pioneering at Antioch, Coretta's sister, Edythe, gave up in disgust and transferred to Ohio State University, which had grown accustomed to Negro faces. By the time Coretta arrived at Antioch, Negro students were no longer rarities, though they were not yet accepted as a matter of course. The problem here was not crass and vulgar bigotry but the day-by-day pinpricks, the stares, the frowns, the little snubs and meannesses that make the "token" Negro's life a guerilla warfare on an undeclared battlefield. As one of a handful of Negro students in a "white" Northern college, Coretta suffered the usual problems of the "token" Negro. Antioch, she has said, was on the whole "the best possible experience for me at the time." But one encounter of these years, an encounter with herself, really, and with her future, gave her pause. When the time arrived for her practice teaching assignment, "the problem" rose up and smote her in the face. Under normal circumstances, she would have been assigned, routinely, to the public school system of Yellow Springs. But no Negro had ever taught there, and some people said no Negro would ever teach there. It is not clear who was responsible for what happened next. Instead of meeting the problem head-on, Coretta's supervisor suggested that she teach instead in the Antioch Demonstration school. Bewildered and hurt, Coretta decided to make an issue of it, saying: "I could have done that in Alabama. I came up here to get away from that kind of thing." True to her word, she carried the fight through channels to the highest authority—all to no avail. Looking back, later, she said: "They were so casual about it. I was so hurt." Thoroughly disillusioned, Coretta sat down and faced herself and her situation. "I told myself: 'This is the problem you have to face. You are a Negro. This is your first experience. This is the first time that it has hit you in the face. You might as well accept the fact.'"

This incident excepted, the Antioch years were broadening for Coretta Scott. And perhaps even this incident played a part in preparing her for the life toward which fate was leading her. Although Coretta was somewhat introspective and withdrawn, she made many friends and received several marriage proposals from Negro and white suitors. She rejected these proposals, feeling that neither she nor her suitors were mature enough. Of one of the white suitors, she said, simply: "I could tell he didn't have the guts. . . ."

Beyond all that was a deeper and more compelling reason. By this time, Coretta was convinced that her future life would revolve around the concert stage. With the recommendations of several persons, including Walter F. Anderson, chairman of the Antioch department of music, she applied to the Jessie Smith Noyes Fund for a fellowship and entered an application at Boston's New England Conservatory of Music. After graduating from Antioch in June, 1951, Coretta spent several anxious weeks awaiting word from the Noyes Foundation. When word did not come, she left for Boston, determined to work there at whatever job she could find until she accumulated enough money to pay her tuition. Fortunately, the fellowship was awarded to her at the last possible moment. The fellowship, however, only covered tuition; there was no money for room and board. Too stubborn to send home for money and too proud to beg, Coretta paid her tuition and went hungry for several days, subsisting on Graham crackers, peanut butter, and fruit. "It was so difficult at first," she said. "For the first time in my life I got hungry." There were elements of irony, even humor, in Coretta's situation. Through a friend, she had secured a room in the home of a wealthy Beacon Hill dowager, a descendant of the Cabots, who let out rooms to talented students. She was starving, therefore, at one of the most fashionable addresses in town. She paid for her lodging and breakfast at the Beacon Hill address by cleaning the fifth floor, three rooms and two stairways. Her immediate problem, therefore, was dinner, which she had missed now for two nights running. At this precise moment, when she was down to her last fifteen cents, a friend who suspected her true plight called and asked her to stop by her home on the way to the conservatory the next day. When Coretta arrived the friend gave her an envelope and said with a pat on the back: "You'll make it. *Of course, you'll make it.*" Coretta opened the envelope on the subway and found fifteen crisp dollars. Tears came to her eyes and words sprang unbidden from her lips. "People are so good," she said. "*Life is so good.*"

After the first year, Coretta's position improved. She started receiving the state aid which Alabama provided for Negroes barred from white institutions of higher learning. She also found a job as a clerk in a mail order house. In the meantime, her vocal studies at the conservatory were progressing, leading some to predict a bright future as a concert artist. And yet, Coretta could not shake the feeling that something was not right with her life. Socially, she was somewhat isolated. Although she had been in Boston several months, she had never met Martin Luther King, Jr., and she knew only a few of the closely-knit Negro student colony. Spiritually, her plight was even more pressing. She said later that she was "searching, looking for something. I was considering joining a new church, either the Unitarians or the Quakers. Martin used to tease me. He used to say that when he met me I had almost gone over." They almost didn't meet. When Mary Powell, a voice student from Atlanta, told Coretta that a young minister from Atlanta wanted to meet her, Coretta said she wasn't interested. The word "minister" did not bring visions of romance and drama and adventure to her mind. She was sure that the Martin Luther King, Jr., Mary Powell praised so highly was "an older man, pious, narrow-minded and not too well-trained, like most of the preachers I had known around my Marion, Alabama, home."

She could not possibly have been further from the truth, as Mary Powell continued to insist. Finally, Coretta gave in, telling Mary Powell that she could give King her telephone number. King called on a Thursday night in February, 1952, and talked for twenty minutes with barely a pause. "There was, as I remember," Coretta recalled, "even mention of Napoleon and Waterloo and stuff like that." Curious, Coretta agreed to meet King on her lunch period the next day.

The meeting began badly. King arrived in his green Chevrolet and Coretta, watching and weighing, decided that he was too short. But the determined young minister regained the initiative, looking Coretta over "so intently" that she became self-conscious. Then, advancing by retreating, King began to discuss not love but communism and capitalism. When Coretta made what she called "some half-way intelligent replies," King's eyes lit up. "Oh," he said, "you can think, too." Later, while driving Coretta home, King said suddenly: "You're everything I'm looking for in a wife." There are only a limited number of answers to a statement of that kind and Coretta, taken aback, could not think of any of them. So she remained silent, wondering now about this strange young man who was unlike any preacher she had ever known. One date led to another and soon Coretta and young Martin were almost inseparable. They went to the movies and to concerts together. Sometimes, they would drive out and buy clams or drop by the Western Lunch Box for King's favorite dish, greens and ham hocks. On occasion, they would just sit and study together. "The more I saw of him," Coretta said, "the more I liked him. There was something about him that sort of grows on you." What impressed her, above all, was King's single-minded determination and his dawning sense of mission. "He talked so often," she said, "about what he planned to do with his life, of what he hoped to contribute to the race and to humanity at large. . . ."

Coretta saw the question coming, and this time she tried to prepare for it. She liked Martin and enjoyed his company, but her plans at the time did not include marriage, certainly not marriage to a minister. In her mind's eye she could see herself dashing across the country, sweeping audiences off their feet, triumphantly taking curtain calls, while tall handsome suitors waited, their arms filled with red roses, at the stage door. She sensed dimly that marriage to a minister would imperil that vision. Moreover, friends at the conservatory told her in no uncertain terms that Martin would never amount to much and that it was foolish, if not immoral, to sacrifice her art to love.

Pushed against the wall of herself, Coretta prayed. Then she asked herself two questions: 1) "Do I love him enough to make any sacrifice?" and 2) "Can I give him up and not miss him?" The answers, she decided, were "yes" in the first instance and "no" in the second.

So, on June 18, 1953, Coretta Scott said "yes" to God and to Martin Luther King, Jr., in a fashionable garden wedding in Heiberger, Alabama. Martin Luther King, Sr., officiated.

After the honeymoon, the couple moved into a four-room apartment near the conservatory. By this time King had completed most of the requirements for the Ph.D. degree. He therefore kept the house and cooked dinner for his student-wife on Thursday evenings.

All this time, on another level, the level of symbols and ideas and words, King was pushing toward the goal engraved on his heart. It was no accident that he chose Boston University for his graduate work in philosophy. As a result of his reading and thinking, he had adopted the philosophical posture of personalism. Boston University at the time was a germinal center of this philosophy, which holds that personality is the key to the meaning of the universe and that not only man but also God is, as King puts it, "supremely personal." At Boston, King studied philosophy and theology under Edgar S. Brightman and L. Harold DeWolf, two of the leading exponents of personal idealism or personalism. "Both men," King has said, "greatly stimulated my thinking. It was mainly under these teachers that I studied personalistic philosophy—the theory that the clue to the meaning of ultimate reality is found in personality. This personal idealism remains today my basic philosophical position. Personalism's insistence that only personality—finite and infinite—is ultimately real strengthened me in two convictions: it gave me metaphysical and philosophical grounding for the idea of a personal God, and it gave me a metaphysical basis for the dignity and worth of all human personality."

With Brightman also, King deepened his understanding of Hegel, mining Hegel's *Phenomenology of Mind* and *Philosophy of Right*. King also took special courses in the Harvard University philosophy department. At Harvard and Boston, King impressed his professors as a young man with a bright future. Dr. DeWolf, head of the department of systematic theology at Boston, has said: "Of all the doctorate students I have had at Boston University—some fifty in all—I would rate King among the top five. Scholastically, he was unusually good."

After completing his course requirements, King settled down to the laborious and lonely job of completing his thesis. He chose as a subject, *A Comparison of the Conceptions of God in the Thinking of Paul Tillich and Henry Nelson Wieman*. As a personal idealist, King disagreed with both Tillich and Wieman, one of whom (Tillich) contended that God was transcendent (i.e., outside things) while the other stressed God's immanence (i.e., His penetration of all things). The collating of the ideas of Tillich and Wieman and the writing of the thesis, which ran to 343 typewritten pages, continued through 1955 and gave King discipline and training in the organization of ideas, if not in the creation of ideas. The latter would come not through books but through an act which began to summon him in the winter of 1953.

Having completed his course requirements, King began, in 1953, to cast about for a place of employment. There was no dearth of opportunities. He had firm offers from at least two Northern churches and invitations from two Southern churches. There were, additionally, offers of a deanship, an administrative position, and a teaching post in three different colleges. As 1953 neared its end, King and his wife looked into the future and tried to discern the signs of fate.

The height of King's ambition at the time was a minister-teacher-prophet career similar to the career of his idol, Benjamin E. Mays, the preacher-president of Morehouse College. Though drawn toward the campus, King decided, and his wife agreed, that it would be wise to enter the academic world, as Mays did, after a successful career as a pastor. The problem before them therefore in this seminal season was a problem of geography—and race. Coretta, who had had enough of the South, was strongly in favor of the proposed Northern pastorates. But King, true to his Black Puritan heritage of *noblesse oblige*, argued passionately for the hard and narrow path of duty, a straight and narrow path that led to the high mountain of fame.

Among the Southern offers before King were "feelers" from the First Baptist Church of Chattanooga, Tennessee, and the Dexter Avenue Baptist Church of Montgomery, Alabama. From the start, King leaned toward Dexter, an upper-income congregation composed largely of professionals and teachers at Alabama State College, the state-supported institution for Negro students. Dexter offered several advantages. As a somewhat intellectual church which frowned on "emotionalism" and "amen-ing," Dexter provided an excellent forum for an ambitious young preacher. Rev. Vernon Johns, the departing Dexter pastor, had made a Southwide reputation as an eloquent and incisive orator and as a fearless advocate of racial justice. The story is told of the time Johns refused to vacate a seat on a Montgomery bus. The bus driver stormed to the rear and shouted: "Nigger, didn't you hear me tell you to get the hell out of that seat?" Johns replied: "And didn't you hear me tell you that I'm going to sit right god-damned here?" The driver, stunned by the rich vocabulary of the well-known minister, retreated in confusion. Repeating this story, word for word, from his pulpit the next Sunday, the Rev. Mr. Johns said he did not believe that God was offended by the unauthorized use of His name. "He probably said," Johns told his congregation, "that I'd better keep an eye on that boy; he's going to do a lot for Christianity down South."

As it turned out, Johns was a John the Baptist to King's Mahatma. In January, 1954, King went to Montgomery to preach a "trial" sermon at Dexter. He preached that morning on "The Three Dimensions of a Complete Life," love of self, love of neighbors, and love of God. Though one woman reportedly said that the twenty-five-year-old minister looked "kind of lost up there without his mother," the majority of the congregation expressed fervent approval. The congregation issued, in April, "a call" for King, who accepted with the understanding that he would not be required to assume full-time duties until the next September. This was acceptable to the congregation and he preached his first sermon as pastor of Dexter in the same month, May, 1954, of the epochal Supreme Court decision on school segregation. For the next four months, King traveled to Montgomery on weekends and returned almost immediately to his Boston apartment or the parental home in Atlanta.

In June, 1954, Coretta Scott King completed her studies at the New England Conservatory of Music; and, in August, the Kings closed their Boston apartment and moved to Atlanta. This marked a sharp break in King's life. After twenty-one straight years in school, he was free to pursue his fortune. King was better prepared than he knew for the trials ahead. In the soil of his youth, and in the house of his father, he had developed an extraordinary flexibility that permitted him to grow with new events and new experiences. No less important were his physical gifts. Though his five-foot-seven frame was hardly impressive, his broad shoulders and muscular neck told of enormous power. There was, moreover, in the oblong, caramel-colored face and the unexpectedly oval eyes something that audiences found piquant. And to these physical gifts must be added the throaty persuasiveness of his baritone voice. The years at Morehouse and Crozer and Boston had broadened these gifts and had taught him how to use them. As he stood now, on the brink of immortality, he was characterized by a forceful intellect, a broad education, a strong capacity for hard work, enormous will power, and a large ambition. The seed was germinable, the seed was viable—and the seed fell not on rock.

Sower

A MUSEUM PIECE of the South's "Lost Cause," Montgomery, Alabama, was chosen by a puckish fate to be the myth-event of the New Cause. The city, which was the first capital of the Confederacy, seemed in 1954 to be a most unlikely place for great events. Schizoid, looking both to the past and to the future, organized around and defined by symbols of defeat and Negro degradation, the city curled around a hairpin bend at the head of the Alabama River. In 1954, there were eighty thousand white citizens. There also lived in Montgomery at the time fifty thousand Negroes. But they were neither citizens nor subjects. To most white people in Montgomery, the Negro populace was composed of objects, tools, instruments, *things* to be manipulated, dominated, and endured.

The Negro community of Montgomery had been subjected over the years to a series of galling indignities. Particularly annoying to Negro leaders was the Montgomery City Lines, a Northern-owned bus company which reportedly insulted Negro citizens though Negro customers contributed almost 70 per cent of the company's revenue. As in practically all Southern cities, bus passengers in Montgomery seated themselves on a segregated, first-come, first-served basis with Negroes seating themselves from the rear forward and whites taking seats from the front backward. In Montgomery, however, unlike some of the more enlightened Southern cities, the first four seats were reserved for the exclusive use of white patrons. Worse, the driver was empowered to order Negroes sitting in the foremost section to yield their seats to white customers. This system, which was a flagrant and open reminder of white supremacy, could not work without a certain amount of tension and unpleasantness. Negro passengers would testify later that it was not unusual for drivers to call them "niggers," "black apes," and "black cows." Nor, it seems, was it unusual for drivers to require Negroes to pay their fares at the front door, get off, and reboard the bus through the rear door. Occasionally, it was said in court, while Negro passengers were going through this complicated ritual, the bus would drive off, leaving them stranded in the middle of the street.

Vernon Johns, Martin Luther King's predecessor at Dexter Avenue Baptist Church, and E. D. (Ed) Nixon, a tough, fearless veteran of Asa Philip Randolph's nonviolent crusade of the forties, had tried desperately to rouse the Negro populace against these and other abuses. All to no avail. By all accounts, the Negro population in 1954 was slumbering fitfully in an uneasy placidity. The Negro population just then was riven geographically and ideologically. And, as always happens when men possess the name of power without the validating instruments, the leaders had fallen into the debilitating habit of fighting each other instead of their oppressors.

To this city, in no whit different from thousands of other Southern towns, came Martin Luther King, Jr., in September, 1954. His charge, the red-brick Dexter Avenue Baptist Church, sat, ironically, at the foot of the mall of the Alabama State Capitol in downtown Montgomery. Near this spot one hundred years before, William Yancey had introduced Jefferson Davis, the new president of the Confederacy, with the words: "The man and the hour have met." In this same place, in the

shadow and ambience of the earlier deed, a new man and a new moment began to approach each other.

Such are the demands of fame that it is likely that the period between September 1, 1954, and December 5, 1955, was one of the happiest—if not the happiest—periods in the life of Martin Luther King,
Jr. In the days before the boycott, the young pastor and his gracious,
charming wife were supremely happy. The couple moved that fall into
the big white frame parsonage at 309 South Jackson Street. The Rev.
Mr. King unpacked his books, put them on the shelves in his study,
and turned from books to face the world.

Following in his father's footsteps, King immediately installed a system of church financing at Dexter similar to the successful Ebenezer
program. (There were no regular collections. Financial contributions
were collected outside the sanctuary.) As the weeks wore away, rounding the curve of winter, King tightened his control over the church and
began to feel the inner joy of a man who finds within himself unsus-
pected reservoirs of leadership. From the beginning, King stressed social action, organizing a social and political action committee within
the church and urging every member to become a registered voter and
a member of the NAACP. Although King had a passion for social justice, his approach to the racial problem at that time was rigidly conventional. He leaned apparently toward the NAACP protest approach,
but he also championed the gradualistic tactics of organizations like the
interracial Alabama Council on Human Relations. This group,
which King served as vice-president, held monthly meetings in the
basement of his church.

Throughout this period, King continued to work on his thesis, writing several hours in the early morning and returning to the task for several hours each night. (He completed the thesis in the spring and was
awarded the Ph.D. degree in systematic theology on June 5, 1955.) No
less important were the hours he spent polishing his sermons. By the
summer of 1955, he had earned a richly deserved reputation as a
preacher and speaker.

Far more fateful and decisive, however, to the subsequent development of his career were events that happened in the outer world. On
May 31, 1955, the Supreme Court ordered school desegregation with
"all deliberate speed." In the wake of this event, White Citizens
Councils sprang up over the South and the atmosphere turned sultry,

darkening with thunderheads of unrest. There then followed an atrocity that cauterized almost all Negroes and prepared them for more
radical departures. On August 28, Emmet Till, a fourteen-year-old
Chicago boy who was vacationing with relatives near Money,
Mississippi, was kidnapped and lynched. The effect of all this on King,
as on so many other Negroes, was explosive. To be sure, King did nothing. Still, he was forced by stirrings within and provocations without to
make an agonizing reappraisal of the Negro situation.

One observes with interest that the things King did not do during
this period were far more important than what he did. The Negro
leadership group in that season was faction-ridden and torn with
controversy. King's inherent decency and a natural instinct of prudence
prevented him from identifying with any particular faction to the
exclusion of the other. With consummate skill, he picked his way
through the undeclared battlefield, winning admiration and later, when
it counted, the votes of moderates, activists, and conservatives.

Another non-act which preserved King for posterity was the declina-
tion of a chance to run for the presidency of the local NAACP
branch. Members of the branch asked him to run for the position
in November, less than a month before the boycott began. King
saw no reason why he should not, but Coretta urged him to turn it
down. She said that his first duty as a new pastor was to organize his
church. Since he was already attending meetings day and night, she
suggested that the NAACP presidency would be "too much." King,
who sometimes defers to his wife's judgment, recalled the incident
later, saying: "Coretta's opposition probably resulted in one of the luck-
iest decisions of my life. For when the bus protest movement broke
out, I would hardly have been able to accept the presidency of the
Montgomery Improvement Association without lending weight to the
oft-made white contention that the whole thing was an NAACP conspiracy."

Into this quiet and conventional life—an hour of philosophical reading in the morning, visits to the sick and infirm, and the usual clerical
round of marrying, baptizing, and burying—came a day in December.
The day, Thursday, December 1, promised to be no better, and no
worse, than any other day. King rose early, as was his wont, read for an
hour, breakfasted, and went about the business of the Lord. W. A.

Gayle, the mayor, rose and went to his office in City Hall. That morning, Rosa Parks, a handsome Negro seamstress in rimless glasses, caught a bus and rode to her job at the Fair department store. In the big frame house on South Jackson, Coretta Scott King changed the baby and put away the breakfast dishes. Time passed, the clock moved, and Montgomery went about its business, livestock, lumber, cotton, fertilizer, the Negroes doing the dirty work, the whites commanding. Cows were killed, buses ran, money was made, prayers were said, babies fed, sins committed, dreams shattered—and through it all, Montgomery marched on to danger, and to destiny.

It was a pleasant day, but unseasonably warm for December. When the downtown stores closed, Negroes and whites thronged the streets, eagerly eyeing the windows, their minds running on to Christmas. There was considerable activity at this hour in Court Square, where; in the days of the Confederacy, Negro slaves had been auctioned. Now, as the early evening haze gathered, a Montgomery City Lines bus pulled through this square and proceeded to its next stop in front of the Empire Theater. On this bus were twenty-four Negroes, including Rosa Parks, who was sitting behind the white section which was filled with twelve white passengers. Six whites boarded the bus at the Empire Theater stop, and the driver left his seat and asked the Negroes in the foremost section to get up and give their seats to the white patrons. This was an ancient custom which excited no undue comment. Three Negroes rose immediately, but Rosa Parks remained seated. The driver again asked her to yield the seat and Rosa Parks, a sweet-tempered, gentle woman, again refused. The driver then summoned police officers, who arrested Rosa Parks for violating the city's segregation ordinances. Because of an extraordinary convergence of forces, because her moment was a crossroad of forces that had been decades in preparation, Rosa Parks' arrest did what no other event, however horrible, had been able to do: it unified and focused the discontent of an entire Negro community. By doing this, by proving that it could be done, the arrest released dammed-up deposits of social energy that rolled across the face of the South and the North. There was, first of all and most important of all, a one-day boycott. The one-day boycott stretched out to 382 days. The 382 days changed the spirit of Martin Luther King, Jr., and King, thus transformed, helped to change the face and the heart of the Negro, of the white man, and of America.

Viewed thus, as a sensitizing social symbol, the Montgomery bus boycott was a myth-event comparable, in a different era and on a smaller
scale, to the French Revolution, of which Kant prophetically said:
"Such a phenomenon in history can never be forgotten, inasmuch as
it has disclosed in human nature the rudiment of and the capacity for
better things which, prior to this, no student of political science had
deduced from the previous course of events."

With Montgomery, an epoch came to an end. To be sure, a new
epoch did not begin immediately. There was an interregnum, a period
of diffuse groping and stumbling. No one knew then, not even King,
which road to take, but it was clear to many that one road, the road of
submission and accommodation, had been closed, perhaps forever.

Why did all this happen?

Why, to go back to the beginning, did Rosa Parks refuse to move?

Martin Luther King, Jr., said later that Rosa Parks had been
"tracked down by the Zeitgeist—the spirit of the times." Rosa Parks, a
former secretary of the local NAACP branch, gave a more prosaic answer. "I don't really know why I wouldn't move. There was no plan at
all. I was just tired from shopping. My feet hurt." At the point where
these two answers coincide is the truth of Montgomery. In the hour of
its beginning, the Negro rebellion was a result of an intersection of
pain—the pain of feet and the deeper, unstated, pain of the heart—
and what William James called "the receptivities of the moment."
There had been pain before, but no Southwide explosion. There had
been bus boycotts before (in Harlem in 1941 and in Baton Rouge in
1953), but no Southwide movement. What made Rosa Parks' pain significant and the Montgomery Bus Boycott compelling was the ambience of the age. Hegel and James apart, Negroes were ready for a new
shuffle of the cards. Events—the interior migration of the thirties and
forties and the convulsion of the fifties—had prepared them. Basic to
an understanding of Montgomery, and of King, is an understanding of
this fact: Negroes had already changed. They only needed an act to
give them power over their fears, an instrument to hold in their hands,
and a man to point the way. Montgomery furnished all three, giving
Negroes not only an act but also a remarkable fisher of men and a
new ideology, nonviolence. Man and method were products and not
causes of the event. It is a point of immense significance that the act

preceded both the man and the idea. King did not seek leadership in Montgomery; leadership sought him. He did not choose nonviolence; nonviolence chose him, imposing itself on him, as it were, as an interior demand of the situation. We can see, with the benefit of hindsight, that it was King, really, that the Zeitgeist was seeking. "Tracked down" and "chosen" by the times, King transcended the occasion, changing the times and transforming a diffuse uprising into a mass movement with passion and purpose. As a catalytic agent, he created a revolutionary point of departure, a new tissue of aspirations and demands. As a magnet and exemplar-myth, as an invitation to a new way of life, King attracted and released the energies of men and women of varying viewpoints.

Beyond all that, King must be seen as a leader who solved a technical problem that had worried Negro leaders for decades. As a powerless group dominated by a powerful majority, Negroes could not stage an open revolt. To go into the streets under those conditions with open demands for change was suicidal. As I have indicated elsewhere, King and the sit-in students solved the technical problems by clothing a national resistance movement in the disarmingly appealing garb of love, forgiveness, and *passive* resistance.

To understand the magnitude of King's accomplishment, it is necessary to understand how he did it, and how much it cost him and others. King, significantly, was marginal to the germination of the Montgomery plot. As pastor of the most influential church in the community, he was, of course, consulted in the feverish hours that followed the Thursday arrest of Rosa Parks. But E. D. Nixon, a Pullman porter, seems to have taken a leading role in the first phase of the controversy which, by Friday night, consumed the attention of diverse strata of the Montgomery Negro community. It was Ed Nixon who arranged Rosa Parks' bail. It was Nixon, King said in his autobiography, who suggested that *something* should be done. After a great deal of telephoning between, among others, the Women's Political Council, Negro professionals, and Negro preachers, including King and Rev. Ralph D. Abernathy of the First Baptist Church, it was decided to stage a one-day bus boycott. Mimeograph machines, without which it is almost impossible to stage a modern rebellion, clanked, and mysterious leaflets appeared on the streets with an anonymous appeal:

Inspecting additions to pool of automobiles used in Montgomery boycott, King talks with Rev. Ralph D Abernathy (l.), Rev. B. J. Sims, and Mrs. Rosa Parks, whose refusal to relinquish bus seat to white man triggered citywide protest.

Mrs. Rosa Parks, a Montgomery seamstress who later
moved to Detroit, Michigan, is fingerprinted after
arrest on December 1, 1955. She was charged with
violation of city segregation code.

Arrested for third time on September 3, 1958, King is
pushed into Montgomery police station by two officers.
King was charged with loitering. He accused police
officers of brutal treatment.

Don't ride the bus to work, to town, to school, or any place Monday, December 5.

Another Negro woman has been arrested and put in jail because she refused to give up her bus seat. . . .

Come to a Mass Meeting, Monday at 7:00 p.m., at the Holt Street Baptist Church for further instruction.

Monday morning came, December 5. King and Coretta rose earlier than usual. A bus stopped a few feet from their door and they were anxious to see the first act in this new and uncharted drama. At this hour, King and other leaders of the Negro community believed they would be lucky to get 60 per cent cooperation. Somewhat apprehensive, fearing a negative response, King and Coretta waited impatiently for the first bus, which usually passed their house at 6 o'clock. King was in the kitchen when Coretta shouted: "Martin! Martin! Come quickly!" King ran to the living room and Coretta pointed to the big orange bus which was inexplicably, gloriously empty. King could hardly believe his eyes but caution checked his joy. It would be better perhaps, he said, to wait for the second bus. But it, too, was empty, or almost; and so was the third. Excited now, envisioning the beginning of a new day, King jumped into his car and drove around the city, scanning the windows of empty buses. An inexpressible joy welled up within him and he told himself that "a miracle" had happened. So it had. That morning, Negroes walked, rode mules, and drove wagons. The boycott was almost totally effective and it would remain so from that December to the next.

One-day social "miracles" are rare; two-day social "miracles" are almost inconceivable, even to ministers. That morning, after Rosa Parks was convicted of violating the city segregation code and fined ten dollars and costs, King and other leading members of the leadership class began to explore the possibilities of a structure that could draw the "miracle" out. Since a mass meeting had already been scheduled for the Holt Street Baptist Church at 7:00 P.M., the leadership group decided to hold an organizational meeting at 3:00 P.M. in the Mount Zion AME Church. At this meeting, it was decided to extend the boycott until the company met certain minimal demands. An *ad hoc* organization, the Montgomery Improvement Association, was formed and Martin Luther King, Jr., was elected president without a dissenting vote. King and others have suggested that King was selected because he was new in the community and was not identified with any faction of the bitterly divided leadership group. It has also been suggested that King was named because almost no one wanted to be identified publicly as the leader of a new departure with an uncertain future.

With only a few minutes remaining before the night mass meeting, King went home to prepare an outline for what he has called "the most decisive speech of my life." It was now six-thirty, and King had only twenty minutes or so to prepare for a venture nothing in Hegel or Rauschenbusch had prepared him for. As the minutes ticked by, he was overwhelmed by a sense of inadequacy. The enormity of the thing, a full-scale Negro rebellion in a Southern town, rose up and smote him in the eyes. As he has done in almost every crisis situation since, King decided through prayer. Then he turned to the outline of his speech only to come face to face with a problem that has always haunted Negro leadership, the problem, as King cogently put it, of how "to make a speech that would be militant enough to keep my people aroused to positive action and yet moderate enough to keep this fervor within controllable and Christian bounds?" King decided finally—and this is a key to his racial philosophy—"to face the challenge head-on," by attempting "to combine two apparent irreconcilables," the militant and the moderate approaches.

When King arrived at the mass meeting, the church was packed and three or four thousand people were standing outside waiting to monitor the proceedings on loudspeakers. This huge crowd voted unanimously to boycott the buses until their demands were met. With billowing enthusiasm, they sang-shouted "Onward Christian Soldiers" and waited patiently as the young Dr. King was introduced. King, speaking without manuscript or notes, reviewed the long train of abuses Negroes had endured on Montgomery buses. He did not quote Gandhi that night, but he did quote Jesus and, remarkably, Booker T. Washington. "Our method," he said, "will be that of persuasion, not coercion. We will only say to the people, 'Let your conscience be your guide.'" He went on to mention the transforming power of love, saying: "Love must be our regulating ideal. Once again we must hear the words of Jesus echoing across the centuries: 'Love your enemies, bless them that curse you, and pray for them that despitefully use you.' If we fail to do this our protest will end up as a meaningless drama on the stage of history, and its memory will be shrouded with the ugly garments of shame. In spite of the mistreatment that we have confronted we must not become bitter, and end up hating our white brothers. As Booker T. Washington said, 'Let no man pull you so low as to make you hate him.' " Then, after the applause died down, King built to a climactic crescendo that would later become his oratorical signature. "If you will protest courageously, and yet with dignity and Christian love, when the history books are written in future generations, the historians will have to pause and say, 'There lived a great people—a black people—who injected new meaning and dignity into the veins of civilization.' This is our challenge and our overwhelming responsibility." As King turned to his seat, the people rose *en masse* in a standing ovation.

So far, so good. There remained now the far more difficult task of inventing and sustaining a structure. In this task, King had the help and support of a doggedly inventive group of aides, most of them ministers, many of them under forty. One of the most talented of this group was Ralph D. Abernathy, a pudgy, pugnacious Baptist minister who selflessly sacrificed his own ambitions in one of the most remarkable acts in the history of Negro leadership. Though markedly different in personality and outlook, King and Abernathy were perfect complements as leaders and as speakers, King taking the high road of philosophy, Abernathy taking the middle road of Baptist fervor, King exalting a crowd with Hegel and Gandhi, Abernathy moving a crowd with humor and earthy examples. Among the other leaders of the boycott directorate were E. D. Nixon, the treasurer, and Fred D. Gray, the young attorney.

Under the impact of these personalities and others, with King serving as an ideologist, spokesman, mediator, and arbiter, the Montgomery Improvement Association became a potent rival of the white city government. Within a short time, a fleet of some three hundred automobiles was making regular runs from forty-six pick-up stations in the community. Equally important, MIA leased space, first in the Negro Baptist Center and finally in the Bricklayers Hall, where Negro Montgomerians trooped with a bewildering variety of problems and requests. To support this immense operation, special collections were taken up in Montgomery Negro churches and at the twice-weekly mass meetings. As word of the boycott spread, donations poured in from all sections of the country and from many countries in Asia and Europe. By the end of the year, the association had disbursed an estimated $225,000.

From the beginning, the Montgomery movement assumed a missionary character. The huge mass meetings, which rotated from church to church, served not only as a means of communication but also as a morale builder. At these meetings, professors, porters, doctors, maids, laborers, housewives, even drunks, abandoned the claims of rank, class, and creed, reaching out to each other in new hope and new faith. Under the impact of the old Negro spirituals, of hand-clapping, shouting, "testifying," and "amen-ing," personality shells dissolved and reintegrated themselves around a larger, more inclusive racial self.

The effect of these meetings on Martin Luther King was no less immediate and obvious. King had tended to look down on the "emotionalism" of the Negro church, but now he began to see that the Negro religious tradition contained enormous reservoirs of psychic and social strength which had never been adequately tapped. And more: King began to accept himself and the Negro people as history had made them, never on that account relaxing the inner demand that he and they should be better. In some such manner, in a church of fire, the re-education, the metamorphosis, of Martin Luther King, Jr., began.

Other transformations were taking place. King had approached the first two negotiating sessions with unwarranted optimism. In truth, the demands of the Negro protestants were modest in the extreme. They asked in the beginning only for courtesy, a first-come, first-served system within the bounds of the segregated system, and the employment of Negro bus drivers on predominantly Negro lines. To King's surprise, city officials and bus officials spurned these "demands," promising only to show "partial" courtesy to Negro customers. It seemed to King and to some neutral observers that some of the officials were more interested in defending the ancient Southern theory that it was not wise, or safe, to give in to a Negro's *demand* as distinguished from a Negro's plea. King had believed that truth would set men free, that Aristotelian logic and the law of the excluded middle would be of some service in the struggle for human justice. Now he saw, with a sinking feeling, that he was wrong, that the issue was not logic but power, that "no one gives up his privileges without strong resistance," and that "the underlying purpose of segregation was to oppress and exploit the segregated, not simply to keep [people] apart."

It was a new man, chastened, who emerged from the negotiating sessions of December 8 and December 18. There was on the opposite side a similar understanding of the tenacity of purpose of the Negro contestants. In the beginning, white Montgomerians—and many Negro Montgomerians—believed that the boycott would eventually unravel at the seams, with the Negro leaders devouring each other like wounded sharks. When this failed to happen, white Montgomery turned mean. The mayor and city commissioners publicly and dramatically joined the White Citizens Council. Finally, on Tuesday, January 24, Mayor Gayle announced what was called a "get-tough" policy. "We have pussy-footed around on this boycott long enough," the mayor said, "and it is time to be frank and honest. . . . The Negro leaders have proved they are not interested in ending the boycott but rather in prolonging it so that they may stir up racial strife. The Negro leaders have proved that they will say one thing to a white man and another thing to a Negro about the boycott. . . . [They] have forced the boycott into campaign between whether the social fabric of our community will continue to exist or will be destroyed by a group of Negro radicals who have split asunder the fine relationships which have existed between the Negro and white people for generations. . . . What they are after is the destruction of our social fabric. . . . The white people are firm in their convictions that they do not care whether the Negroes ever ride a city bus again if it means that the social fabric of our community is destroyed so that Negroes will start riding buses again."

There then followed a series of incidents that strained Montgomery's "social fabric" to the breaking point and projected Martin Luther King into the national spotlight. In the early days of the boycott, it was by no means certain that King would emerge as the leader of the movement. Speculation tended rather to revolve around Ralph Abernathy, Fred Gray, and other professionals who had been in the community longer than King. Forty-five days after the boycott began, Tom Johnson, a Montgomery reporter, asked editorially, "Who is the acknowledged boycott leader?" Johnson said that it "seemed" to be King, but the question could only be answered, as it was answered, in an act.

On Thursday afternoon, January 26, as a direct result apparently of the "get-tough" policy, King was arrested on a charge of driving thirty miles an hour in a twenty-five mile zone. Two policemen searched the young pastor, pushed him into a patrol car, and drove away. King, who had never been arrested before and who had not the vaguest idea of the location of the city jail, noticed that the car drove away from the downtown section where he assumed the jail was located. For a moment he panicked, sure that the officers were carrying him to an isolated spot for mayhem or even murder. He was therefore relieved when the car arrived at the jail where he was thrown into a cell with drunks, thieves, murderers, and vagrants.

If, as Tolstoy said, "nobody knows what kind of government it is who has never been in prison," then the first arrest of Martin King must certainly be listed as one of the most educational experiences of his life. Stunned into speechlessness, King surveyed the crowded cells, noticing the dehumanizing atmosphere, the men lying sprawled on mattresses, slats, even the floor; the open, revoltingly nauseous toilets, and everywhere the psychic fever of men dehumanized by being caged in such conditions or by caging men in that condition. King told himself and would later tell others that "no matter what these men had done, they shouldn't be treated like this." Fortunately, King did not remain long in jail. When a large number of Negroes assembled before the jail, the jailer decided that justice would be served if King were permitted to sign his own bond. Just before King left the jail, one of his cellmates said: "Don't forget us when you get out."

Four days later, on Monday, January 30, while King was addressing a mass meeting, a bomb was thrown on the porch of his home. When the bomb landed, Coretta, who was talking to the wife of a church member in the living room, told herself that it was only a brick. But "somehow," she said, "I felt that we should go to the back." When they were halfway to the back, the bomb exploded, splitting a pillar on the porch, shattering the front windows and filling the living room with a hail of broken glass. To Coretta, the blast sounded as though it had blown the whole front of the house away. She could feel the cold air surging through the house, and she thought, "Well, it finally happened." Her next thought was of her nine-week-old baby, sleeping in a bassinet in the back room. For a moment, she paused, not knowing quite what to do, trying to think of someone to call. Then she and Mrs. Roscoe Williams went into the bedroom. At that moment, the doorbell rang. "My first thought," Coretta King said, "was that they are coming in now. And for a split second, I got a little panicky wondering what to do about the baby. Finally, a voice said: 'Is anybody hurt?' I knew then they were friendly callers. I went up front. . . . There was smoke everywhere. Then the telephone started ringing. Somebody answered and a woman said: 'Yes, I did it. And I'm just sorry I didn't kill all you bastards.' Then people from all over town started gathering."

When King arrived, some fifteen minutes later, the house was ringed by an angry Negro crowd armed with guns, rocks, rods, knives, sticks, and Coca-Cola bottles. As he pushed his way through the crowd, he heard a Negro bystander tell a white policeman: "Now, you got your .38 and I got mine; so let's battle it out." King went into the house, which was filled now with policemen, firemen, and other guardians of law and order including the fire chief and Mayor Gayle. He talked briefly with his wife, looked in on the baby, and returned to the front where the crowd was trembling on the verge of a violent and apocalyptic spasm. By now, it was 9:30 or thereabouts, and more than one thousand Negroes were milling in the street in front of the house. King stood on the front porch for a moment, studying the crowd. At his side were the mayor and other city officials, their faces graven with anxiety and apprehension. It was clear to almost everyone that Montgomery was on the verge of a blood bath and it seemed then that there was nothing anyone could do about it. Shouts, threats, curses rent the air. Only a spark was needed to inflame the crowd, which had been driven to the edge of desperation by repeated acts of insult. Uneasily aware of that fact, King raised his arms. "Don't get panicky," he said. "Don't do anything panicky at all. Don't get your weapons. He who lives by the sword will perish by the sword." As the crowd fell silent, wondering at these words coming from the lips of a man whose wife and child had narrowly escaped serious injury and perhaps death, King rushed on: "We are not advocating violence. I want you to love our enemies. Be good to them. Love them and let them know you love them. I did not start this boycott. I was asked by you to serve as your spokesman. I want it to be known the length and breadth of the land that if I am stopped, this movement will not stop. If I am stopped, our work will not stop, for what we are doing is right. What we are doing is just and God is with us." As King finished, cries of "amen" and "God bless you, son" floated up from the crowd, which began to disperse, its anger deflected, dissipated.

This moment changed the course of the protest and made King a living symbol. He and other members of the boycott directorate had spoken before of love and forgiveness. But now, *seeing the idea in action*, fleshed out by pain, paid for by anguish, millions were touched, if not converted. The parable of the porch went out now over the wires of the news media and King's name became a token to almost all American Negroes. Of greater immediate consequence, however, was the impact of the event on the Montgomery movement, of which King now became leader, not only by election but also by the acclamations of committed hearts.

Though King spoke persuasively that night of love and forgiveness, he was not yet a Gandhian. Later that night, in a quieter moment, the claims of manhood reasserted themselves. Reliving the moment, realizing that his wife and baby could have been killed, he was filled with rage. The indignity of it, the insult of it, the "viciousness of people" who would deliberately, consciously, cold-bloodedly perform a series of operations designed to snuff out his life, and the lives of his wife and nine-week-old baby: all this overwhelmed him and drove him to the "verge of corroding hatred." Lying in the bed, King wrestled with himself and overcame himself, saying: "You must not allow yourself to become bitter." Still, King was more than half receptive when someone suggested that self-defense was the better part of valor. With friends, he went to the sheriff's office and applied for a gun permit. The application was finally denied. By that time, however, King was convinced that even self-defense was wrong. He came to this view by a roundabout route. Contrary to the common impression, he did not enter the Montgomery struggle with a vision of battle. Somewhere in the back of his mind, of course, were the seeds of his 1950 perusal of Gandhism. But it would be an error to conclude from this that the King of 1955 was a Gandhian. The truth is at once more prosaic and more striking: *Martin King convinced himself and, in convincing himself, he convinced others.*

In the beginning, nothing apparently was further from the minds of Montgomery resistants than Mahatma Gandhi. King and other leaders urged Negro boycotters to remain calm and peaceful but they relied primarily on the words of Jesus and the traditional Negro leadership rhetoric that Negroes could never win in America with violence.

Although the leaders stressed peaceful protest, they also believed apparently in the Western tradition of self-defense, as witness King's application for a gun permit.

Interestingly enough, in his first major interviews with Robert E. Johnson, a college classmate who was the managing editor of *Jet*, and Tom Johnson, a white Montgomery reporter, King did not mention Gandhi at all. In the Tom Johnson interview, published January 19, 1956, in the *Montgomery Advertiser*, King said he was motivated chiefly by the "social gospel." "Besides the religious philosophers," Tom Johnson reported, "King was particularly interested in the German philosophers Kant and Hegel. The latter, his favorite, fathered the 'dialectical process' which holds that change is the cardinal principle of life and that in every stage of things there is a contradiction which only the 'strife of opposites' can resolve."

Paradoxically, the idea for an opening to Gandhi seems to have come from a Southern white woman. Soon after the boycott began, Juliette Morgan, a white Montgomery librarian, remarked, in a letter to the editor of the *Montgomery Advertiser*, on the similarities between the Montgomery struggle and Gandhi's crusade. The leaders, who were moving in a similar direction, seized on this idea and began to use Gandhi as an authority in their frequent appeals for restraint. The Gandhi idea caught on, particularly and at first almost exclusively with the large number of Northern and European reporters who flocked to the scene.

The opening to Gandhi was facilitated by two factors: King's propensity—largely because of his philosophical training and his original choice of himself as a symbolic being—for large ideas and concepts; and the further fact that the movement was already based on the solid rock of the Negro religious tradition. What King did now—and it was a huge achievement—was to turn the Negro's rooted faith in the church to social and political account by melding the image of Gandhi and the image of the Negro preacher and by overlaying all with Negro songs and symbols that bypassed cerebral centers and exploded in the well of the Negro psyche.

Nonviolence, as we have seen, was not a new idea in the ghetto or in America. Ninety-eight years before King was born, and some eighty years before Gandhi's first campaign, William Lloyd Garrison, the white abolitionist, made what was perhaps the first sustained attempt to use passive resistance as an instrument of liberation in a major social conflict. Garrison used much the same phrases Gandhi and, later, King would use. "The history of mankind," he said, "is crowded with evidences proving that physical coercion is not adapted to moral regeneration; that the sinful disposition of man can be subdued only by love; that evil can be exterminated from the earth only by goodness; . . . that there is great security in being gentle, harmless, long-suffering, and abundant in mercy; that it is only the meek who shall inherit the earth, for the violent who resort to the sword are destined to perish with the sword."

Nonviolence was not only ancient; it was also a submerged, though far from articulate, element in the world view of the Negro leadership class, which could not visualize any practical alternative. "We must condemn physical force and banish it from our minds," James Weldon Johnson said. "But I do not condemn it on any moral or pacific grounds. The resort to force remains and will doubtless always remain the rightful recourse of oppressed peoples. Our own country was established upon that right. I condemn physical force because I know that in our case it would be futile." Though, as this quote indicates, the nonviolent strain in the Negro leadership tradition was more practical than theoretical, the graveyard of Negro leadership was by 1956 replete with the bones of men who had attempted to establish an American passive resistance movement based on Gandhian methodology. The matter was discussed seriously in the twenties after Gandhi launched his Indian campaign. In a 1924 symposium in the *Crisis*, the NAACP journal, several Negro leaders and intellectuals debated the possibilities of a duplication on American soil of Gandhi's struggle. E. Franklin Frazier, the Negro sociologist, seems to have expressed the majority view, saying there would be a "blood bath" if a Gandhi arose to lead Negroes. As a sociologist, Frazier was contemptuous of the redemptive power of love. "If the masses of Negroes can save their self-respect and remain free of hate, so much the better for their moral development. [But] I believe it would be better for the Negro's soul to be seared with hate than dwarfed by self-abasement."

Despite these negative assessments, the idea of an American Gandhi persisted, fueled by the glowing reports of Howard Thurman, then

dean of the Howard University Chapel, and other Negroes who made
pilgrimages to India and to Gandhi. Finally, in the turbulent forties,
Asa Philip Randolph electrified Negro America with a broad-scale attempt to create a mass-based civil disobedience movement. Stimulated
by John L. Lewis' success with sit-down strikes and massive unrest in
Negro ghettos, Randolph called for a "nonviolent goodwill direct action campaign," including school and bus boycotts, mass marches on
city halls and the White House. Buoyed up by the response, Randolph
staged in 1942 a series of mass meetings of a size and intensity unpar-
alleled in the ghetto. Then disaster struck. On the eve of the proposed
"civil disobedience campaign," America erupted in the violent riot season of 1943. Chastened, Randolph and his aides "postponed" the campaign and it was never revived.

   Though the "American Gandhi," as Randolph was called, failed in
his main objectives, he did activate new charges of energy, influencing
Bayard Rustin, Daisy Bates, E. D. Nixon, and others. More concretely, the new idea was institutionalized with the founding in 1942
of CORE. This organization grew out of a memorandum, "Provisional
Plan for Brotherhood Mobilization," which James Farmer, a young
pacifist, submitted to A. J. Muste and the Fellowship of Reconciliation on February 19, 1942. Farmer proposed a "creative" application of
Gandhian tactics to the American race problem, avoiding, however,
"an uncritical duplication of the Gandhian steps in organization and
execution." The heart of his plan was a national mobilization extending over a five- or ten-year period "after which, it is to be hoped,
relentless non-cooperation, economic boycott, civil disobedience,
et cetera, will be thrown into swing wherever and whenever possible."
CORE, with Farmer as its first national director, succeeded in staging
a small "Freedom Ride" in 1947 and integrated public facilities in several Northern and border states, but the "relentless non-cooperation
. . . et cetera" Farmer envisioned had to await the maturing of events
and of Martin Luther King, Jr.

   All these currents, which had been swirling for years beneath the
surface of Negro life, began to converge on Montgomery and Martin
Luther King, Jr., in the early months of 1956. By that time, two Negro-
Americans—Adam Clayton Powell in Marching Blacks (1945) and
Howard Thurman in Jesus and the Disinherited (1949)—had written
books on nonviolence and the Negro struggle. (King read or reread at
least one of these books, Jesus and the Disinherited, after the boycott

began.) The Fellowship of Reconciliation and CORE also had considerable experience with nonviolent direct action and soon after the boycott began, members of these groups, Bayard Rustin and A. J. Muste among others, drifted into town with advice and patterned programs.

As the boycott wore on, King plunged ever deeper into Gandhism. A post-boycott trip to India, in 1959, solidified his commitment to the cause. Even more decisive perhaps in the transformation of King was a ministry of pain. The pressures on King and his wife grew apace as his fame spread. In 1956-57, the frame house on South Jackson Street became a vortex of swirling forces that threatened to engulf the minister and his young wife. Day and night the phone jangled, bringing oftentimes violent and abusive threats. Wherever King went, wherever he traveled, in Montgomery or in the Northern cities to which he went often now to make fervently received speeches, the demands of developing fame claimed him, turning, twisting, altering his life in a spiraling pattern of pressure. Hovering over all, subtly shaping and distending all was the ever present possibility of sudden and violent death. Stretched taut on the rack of himself, having no time to sort out, analyze and organize the new experiences through which he was going, King came one night in January, 1956, to the end of his personal rope. The air was thick with doubts and very real dangers then, and King, sitting dejected in the kitchen of his home, told God that he couldn't go any further alone. "I am here taking a stand for what I believe is right," he said, "but now I am afraid. The people are looking to me for leadership, and if I stand before them without strength and courage, they too will falter. I am at the end of my powers. I have nothing left. I've come to the point where I can't face it alone." Into King's kitchen, or so it seemed to him at any rate, came "the presence of the Divine," and he thought he heard the "quiet assurance of an inner voice saying: 'Stand up for righteousness, stand up for truth; and God will be at your side forever.'" This "vision," which bore the mark not of Gandhi but of the Negro Baptist tradition was, as King admitted, a turning point in his life. Having reached the end of himself, he now began to experience the beginning of himself. After that experience, King said in his autobiography, "My uncertainty disappeared. I was ready to face anything."

Building on the Gandhi tradition, learning not so much from words as words fed by the blood of experience, King now transformed himself and the Montgomery movement, giving men, women, children, and himself a new vision of struggle and a new vision of the possibilities of man. King has said that the *experience* of Montgomery "did more to clarify my thinking on the question of nonviolence than all the books that I have read." He also said that the spirit of the Montgomery movement came from Jesus, the technique from Gandhi.

The Montgomery struggle continued throughout the year of 1956 but it was won, really, at the point where King and, through him, the Negro population cast off fear, saying with their spirit and, most importantly, with their bodies, that they were ready to *lose* everything in order to win. Not understanding the depth of change in the Negro community, the white power structure made extraordinary blunders. On February 21, for example, the Montgomery County Grand Jury indicted some ninety of the leading boycott participants on a charge of violating a 1921 statute which made it a misdemeanor for anyone to hinder lawful business without "just cause or legal excuse." Within forty-eight hours King and other leading pastors were arrested. The mass arrest of practically all the Negro ministers of Montgomery, as almost anyone could have predicted, unified the Negro community as it had never been unified before; and the trial of King, as a test case for the other indicted Montgomerians, served only to increase his stature, locally and nationally.

During the four-day trial, the Negroes of Montgomery thronged the courtroom, wearing cloth crosses bearing the legend: "Father, forgive them." When King was convicted on March 22, he and Coretta emerged from the courtroom, smiling triumphantly. On the courthouse steps, the young couple was hailed by a large crowd of demonstrators, shouting: "Long live the King! We ain't gonna ride the buses no more."

All the while, on another level, the legal level, things of consequence were unfolding. Under the impact of events, the movement jettisoned its original demands and opened an attack on segregation *per se*. On February 1, four Negro women asked the federal court to ban bus segregation in Montgomery. On June 4, the court ruled that statutes requiring bus segregation in Montgomery were illegal. The case was immediately appealed to the United States Supreme Court. Before that tribunal could hand down a decision, Montgomery officials made a grab for victory that almost succeeded, asking a state court to enjoin the Montgomery Improvement Association from operating an illegal transit system. This move, of course, imperiled not only the car pool but also the movement. On Tuesday, November 13, King and his aides, their spirits drooping, waited forlornly in a Montgomery court-room for the inevitable decision outlawing the car pool. During a lull in the proceedings, King noticed a stir at the prosecution table. At that moment, Rex Thomas, an Associated Press reporter, handed King a piece of paper on which these words were written:

> The United States Supreme Court today affirmed a decision of a special three-judge U.S. District Court in declaring Alabama's state and local laws requiring segregation on buses unconstitutional.

The word sped through the crowd. From somewhere in the court-room came the booming voice of an anonymous Negro: "God Almighty has spoken from Washington, D.C." The next night, Wednesday, November 14, some ten thousand Negroes, holding simultaneous meetings in two churches, voted to end the boycott. King asked his followers to go back to the buses "with humility and meekness." "I would be terribly disappointed," he said, "if any of you go back to the buses bragging, "We, the Negroes, won a victory over the white people. . . ." Of the 382-day struggle which he would later call "one of the greatest in the history of the nation," King said: "All along, we have sought to carry out the protest on high moral standards . . . rooted in the deep soil of the Christian faith. We have carefully avoided bit-terness. [The] months have not at all been easy . . . Our feet have often been tired and our automobiles worn, but we have kept going with the faith that in our struggle we had cosmic companionship, and that, at bottom, the universe is on the side of justice. [The Supreme Court decision was] a revelation of the eternal validity of this faith, [and] came to all of us as a joyous daybreak to end the long night of enforced segregation in public transportation."

On Friday, December 21, after receipt of the Supreme Court order, the Montgomery buses were integrated, with King and a party consisting of E. D. Nixon and the Rev. Glenn Smiley, a white minister, leading. After a spasm of violence, including the bombing of four Negro churches and the homes of Ralph D. Abernathy and other leaders, Montgomery came to a grudging peace with Martin King's *Zetgieist*.

It is a point of immense interest that the Montgomery movement began in irony and ended in irony. It began not as a protest against segregation but as a demand for more equal treatment within the "separate-but-equal" system; and it ended not as a triumph of passive resistance but as a confirmation of the NAACP theory that lawyers are the Negro's best friend. And yet, when all this is said, one fact remains: Montgomery transcended lawyers. There was an incident at the mass meeting celebrating the end of the struggle that is very illuminating in this general connection. The Rev. Robert Graetz, the only white man in the leadership of the movement, decided that night to read the scripture according to Paul: "When I was a child, I spoke as a child, I understood as a child, I thought as a child. . . ." At this point, there was a vast uproar. All over the floor now, men and women were on their feet, waving handkerchiefs and weeping. It was only with great difficulty that Graetz completed the sentence.

> . . . But when I became a man, I put away childish things.

The Negro people had grown, tremendously; and so had Martin Luther King, Jr. In the days ahead King and the Negro people would grow together, reciprocally influencing each other, King contributing to the radicalization of the Negro people and the growing radicalization of the Negro people pushing King to new postures, the whole process pushing upward and outward in an ascending curve of resistance.

When the Montgomery boycott ended, King was only twenty-seven years old. A little below average height, his oblong face purified by a long looking on death and on evil, King presented a picture of deliberative determination. Like Booker T. Washington, who was famous at thirty-nine, and Frederick Douglass, who was internationally known at twenty-eight, King stood on the heights at an early age. Despite his age, King, like Douglass, was well prepared for the task assigned him by history. An excellent orator, getting better with every delivery, King had an ability, rare in Negro leadership circles, to articulate and dramatize ideas. He also had a superb sense of history. Moreover, King had, as he had just demonstrated in Montgomery, an unexcelled ability to pull men and women of diverse viewpoints together and to keep their eyes focused on the goals. It was said on the debit side that King was deficient in administrative ability. He himself admitted that details bored him, a fact which does not concern us here. It cannot be said too often that administration is one thing, and leadership another. Brilliant administrators are born several times every day; a man with King's genius, with his ability to move men and motivate them, is born once a generation, if not once a century. If King were an administrator, if he had been blessed and cursed with the bureaucratic sensibility, a sensibility given to caution and an overemphasis on the rituals of paperwork, he would not have triumphed in Montgomery and we would not be discussing him here. What is important is that King, like Franklin Delano Roosevelt, demonstrated in Montgomery and later a rare talent for attracting and using the skills and ideas of brilliant aides and administrators. Of greater weight than the charge of administrative fumbling was the criticism, that grew in force in the sixties, that there was a certain softness, a certain fuzziness and lack of focus in King's leadership, a deficiency that stemmed, or so the critics said, from the fact that he tended to make ends of his means.

King emerged from the boycott as a national leader with a popular backing of a depth and intensity unknown in America since the days of Booker T. Washington. His increasing weight in the world of men was obvious even before the end of the boycott. On May 17, 1956, for example, he was invited to speak at the Cathedral of St. John the Divine in New York City. In August, he appeared before the platform committee of the Democratic National Convention. By the spring of 1957, he was one of America's most sought-after speakers and his name was known in almost every corner of America. Time, the leading white-oriented news magazine, and Jet, the leading Negro-oriented news magazine, had run cover stories on him. Long and generally approving articles had appeared in almost every large American periodical and most major newspapers abroad. The general tenor of these articles can be gauged by the Jet article which said King had become "a symbol of divinely inspired hope," "a kind of modern Moses who has brought new self-respect to Southern Negroes."

The trickle of tributes became a flood in 1957. In May, King became the youngest person and the first active pastor to win the Spingarn Medal, which is awarded annually to the person making the largest contribution in the field of race relations. The next month, in June, he received the first of his scores of honorary degrees. Particularly pleasing to King was the citation from Morehouse, his alma mater. Speaking with great feeling, Benjamin E. Mays said:

> You are mature beyond your years, wiser at twenty-eight than most men at sixty; more courageous in a righteous struggle than most men can ever be; living a faith that most men preach about and never experience. Significant, indeed, is the fact that you did not seek the leadership in the Montgomery controversy. It was thrust upon you by the people. You did not betray that trust of leadership. You led the people with quiet dignity, Christian grace, and determined purpose. While you were away, your colleagues in the battle for freedom were being hounded and arrested like criminals. When it was suggested by legal counsel that you might stay away and escape arrest, I heard you say with my own ears: "I would rather spend ten years in jail than desert the people in this crisis." At that moment, my heart, my mind, and my soul stood up erect and saluted you. I knew then that you were called to leadership for just such a time as this. . . . On this our 90th anniversary, your Alma Mater is happy to be the first college or university to honor you this way.

Then, his voice trembling with emotion, Benjamin E. Mays executed one of the oratorical flourishes that had drawn King into the ministry ten years before. "See," Benjamin Mays said, quoting Emerson, "how the masses of men worry themselves into nameless graves when here and there a great soul forgets himself into immortality."

All this was heady wine which could have destroyed a man with less balance. Despite his stolidity, King did not escape—no one could have escaped—unscathed. He is said to have complained in 1957 that he hadn't read a new book, thought a new thought, or made a new speech in a year. More significantly, he confessed to the inevitable crisis of identity. He was not in January of 1957 the same man he was in January of 1956. But who was he? And what did he want now, now that he could have almost anything he wanted? Offers by the dozen poured into the South Jackson house in the days after the boycott, ten-, fifteen-, twenty-thousand-dollar-a-year offers, the pastorship of a large Northern white church, professorships and even a deanship of major white universities. Even more tempting were opportunities to earn more than $75,000 a year as a professional lecturer. "Frankly," King told J. Pius Barbour, an old friend, "I'm worried to death. A man who hits the peak at twenty-seven has a tough job ahead. People will be expecting me to pull rabbits out of the hat for the rest of my life."

Fame being marketable, many men came to Montgomery to tell King who he was and where he should want to go. King, as usual, listened patiently and kept his counsel, waiting for events to speak to him. Either through events or through the working of his exquisitely tuned personal radar, he decided finally that he was, first, a pastor, and, second, a Negro leader or, at least, a Southern Negro leader. He said then and would say later that the second was an extension and not an addition to the first.

During the year which was now behind King but which somehow would never leave him, traits in his character had hardened and new sensitivities had emerged. As a result of his immersion in the church of fire, King had come to radically different conclusions about the nature of the Negro struggle. A key concept in his new orientation was the idea of confrontation, the idea of bringing out into the open submerged evils, of *forcing* face-to-face meetings of man and man, of community and community, individually as in the refusal of a single individual to accept segregation, collectively as in the open challenge by a Negro community of the fiats and fears of a white community. The idea that nothing substantial would happen in the field of race relations if men and communities were not *forced* to face evils was stated with great eloquence by Asa Randolph in the forties, but King carried it to a higher stage of development, making the "showdown situation" the central component of the Negro's new vision of battle. Like Randolph, he believed direct action indispensable for racial progress. "Pressure, even conflict," he said, "was an unfortunate but necessary element in social change." Abandoning the mainstream Negro leadership tradition, which shied away from conflict and considered direct appeals to the masses inflammatory, King called for a total mobilization of all the resources in the Negro community—"the no D's and the Ph.D's." He stressed, moreover, the responsibility of every individual to history in the making. Every individual, according to King, had a right, nay, a duty, to break or ignore unjust laws. Any man who accepted segregation involved himself, tragically, in his own degradation.

A practical idealist, fervent in exhortation but cool and circumspect in action, King fashioned his neo-Gandhian philosophy over a four-year period extending through the fall of 1961. Like James Farmer, he argued against an "uncritical duplication" of Gandhism. The Gandhian program as it evolved during the Indian struggle included collective civil disobedience, hartals, work stoppages, etc., based on an absolute turning away from the government and a refusal to recognize its authority or even its existence. King stopped far short of collective civil disobedience. In 1957, he only advocated the right of individuals acting as individuals to violate "unjust local laws" that conflicted with national laws. "Every man," he said, "has a right and personal responsibility to break, ignore and resist certain local laws—no matter what the personal consequences are—in order to abide by the national law." As for collective action similar to the Montgomery struggle, King said: "All cities have conditions that could lead to the kind of thing we are doing in Montgomery. I would not, however, advocate the indiscriminate use of the boycott as a weapon. Whenever it is tried, the Negro must be sure that it is well-organized, strategically wise, and in an area where counter-boycotts cannot be used against them." Despite the limitations King placed on passive resistance, his contention that Negroes had a right to disobey local segregation laws had revolutionary implications.

With the formation of the Southern Christian Leadership Conference (SCLC), King became an institution. Sixty Negro leaders, most of them preachers, from ten Southern states founded the organization at a meeting in Atlanta's Ebenezer Baptist Church on January 10-11, 1957. The next month at a meeting in New Orleans the organization, which was then known as the Southern Conference on Transportation and Nonviolent Integration, changed its name and elected King president. SCLC in its original call to battle reflected King's ideas, calling upon all Negroes, "to assert their human dignity" by refusing "further cooperation with evil." "But far beyond this," the organization said, "we call upon them to accept Christian love in full knowledge of its power to defy evil. We call upon them to understand that nonviolence is not a symbol of weakness or cowardice, but as Jesus demonstrated, non-violent resistance transforms weakness into strength and breeds courage in the face of danger."

In its formative years, the organization, as its first name indicated, was concerned primarily with segregation in transportation facilities and voter registration. Some of the more theoretical sit-in students would say later that the Montgomery idea was aborted before it reached full development. While there is some truth in this, it is surely true also that the foundation of the movements of the sixties was laid by King's first strides in the darkness of the new departure.

Future consequence apart, King's ideas had immediate effects. With the crystallization of King's ideas in the Southern Christian Leadership Conference and their diffusion through articulate strata of the Negro community, a sense of urgency penetrated Negro leaders. Lewis W. Jones has called attention to this fact in an important essay on the Tuskegee movement. "In the spring of 1957," he wrote, "strong sentiment developed among Tuskegee Negroes to 'do something about our situation.' Outspoken persons within and without the Tuskegee Civic Association talked about something 'similar to the action taken in nearby Montgomery regarding the public transportation boycott.'" This feeling—the feeling that it was necessary "to do something"— and its corollary—the implicit threat that if Negro men of power did not "do something" somebody else would—opened fissures in several Negro communities and prepared the way for a displacement of accommodating Negro leadership. More significantly, young Negro preachers began to view themselves through the prism of the King image. The grand outcome was a series of bus boycotts in Tallahassee, Atlanta, and other communities. When, in January, 1959, Atlanta's buses were desegregated, the Rev. William Holmes Borders said, "Thank you, Montgomery. Thank you, Martin Luther King, Jr." King's influence was also perceptible in Little Rock, where Daisy Bates, a state NAACP leader, outmaneuvered state and city officials and kept nine Negro children in a school which had become a national battleground.

The adulation which King received in 1957 cannot be explained entirely by King's acts. It must be explained, at least in part, by what men and women saw in King. For some fifty years, Negroes had been expecting a leader. Now, as King's image rose on the horizon, Negroes of all ranks and creeds pooled their psychic energy and projected it onto King, anxiously asking themselves, anxiously asking King, with

After indictment by Montgomery County Grand Jury on charge of participating in illegal boycott, King, accompanied by Abernathy, is booked by police officer.

King completes formalities by posing for police "mug" photo. King and eighty-nine boycott leaders and participants were indicted under 1921 state law which made it illegal to hinder a lawful business without "just" cause.

Emerging from Montgomery court after March, 1956, conviction on illegal boycott charge, King and wife are hailed by supporters. King said judge had "started a fire he couldn't stop."

Leaving Montgomery jail after posting bond on charges stemming from filing of his state income tax returns, King is flanked by aides, reporters and Attorney W. Robert Ming (left, forefront).

every gesture, every glance: "Art thou he who should come or should we seek another?"

No serious student of King's life can help being struck by what can only be called the genius of his unconscious. Like all great men, he seems to have a talent for appearing at the right fork on the right road. It was his good fortune in 1957 to appear on the national scene at a time when lines of forces that had been gathering since his birth were coming to an intersection. Since the early twenties, American Negroes had been gathering fury against their situation, and impersonal socio-economic forces—urbanization, a developing middle class, the rise of the welfare state, etc.—had heightened their hopes and sharpened their sensitivities. Postwar developments, particularly the Supreme Court decision of 1954 and the crumbling of European colonialism, had dangerously increased Negro aspirations. Now, in 1957, in the wake of Southern resistance to the Supreme Court decision and a deepening economic crisis in Northern ghettos, Negroes were becoming increasingly restive over mainstream leadership tactics of protest and appeal. And out of this there began to emerge the feeling, nebulous at first but always waxing clearer, that another line had to be found. A feeling began to creep from Negro to Negro in these years, from ghetto to ghetto, a dawning sense, a fiery hope, that things did not have to be that way forever, that someway, *somehow* life could be better. For having sensed that hope, long before he knew what to do with it, and long before others could name it, Martin Luther King, Jr., earned the right from 1957 on to speak for the Negro, and for man.

That fact became obvious during the Prayer Pilgrimage of May 17, 1957, an event and a date that marked King's entree into the field of national Negro leadership. Although King shared the leadership of this event with Asa P. Randolph and Roy Wilkins, the NAACP executive secretary, it was clear from the crowd's response that King was the man of the hour. It was he who dominated the headlines; it was he who stirred the thirty-five thousand pilgrims who came from thirty states to stand before the Lincoln Monument in the largest civil rights demonstration yet organized. The demonstrators listened patiently and in some cases enthusiastically to a vast array of speakers, including Wilkins, Randolph, and Adam Clayton Powell; but their hearts went out to King. When Randolph introduced King, the crowd came to its feet, waving white handkerchiefs and programs. King, wearing a black robe, looking even younger than his twenty-eight years, stood silent for a moment, staring out over the crowd that pressed at the foot of the memorial steps and flared out into the park on each side. Then, speaking slowly, he launched into his address, buoyed up by the spontaneous chorus of "amens" that sounded at the end of each salient thrust. In this, his first truly national address, King arraigned both political parties for "betraying" the cause of justice. The executive department of the government, then headed by Dwight David Eisenhower, was "too şilent and apathetic," he said, and the legislative branch was "too stagnant and hypocritical." What then did he propose? There was a need, he said, for leadership on four fronts. First, there was a need for strong, aggressive leadership from the federal government. There was a need also for strong leadership from white liberals who were bogged down in "a sort of quasi-liberalism, based on the principle of looking sympathetically at all sides." Beyond all that, King said, there must be "strong leadership from the white moderates of the South, and strong, courageous, and intelligent leadership from the Negro community." All this was sound as the words of the Gospel; but toward what end should strong leadership aspire, and with what means? King, who had won fame in a direct-action attack on public accommodations, chose now, probably for tactical reasons connected with his emerging entente with the Negro power structure, to emphasize voter registration. In a rhythmically compelling flight of oratory which immediately established an antiphonal relation between speaker and audience, King shouted: "Give us the ballot and we will no longer plead—we will write the proper laws on the books. Give us the ballot and we will fill the legislature with men of goodwill. Give us the ballot and we will get the people judges who love mercy. Give us the ballot and we will quietly, lawfully, implement the May 17, 1954, decision of the Supreme Court. . . . Give us the ballot and we will transform the salient misdeeds of the bloodthirsty mobs into the calculated good deeds of orderly citizens." King went on to speak of the trials of Montgomery, of the bombings and acts of terror. But, said he, "we must never be bitter —if we indulge in hate, the new order will only be the old order. . . . We must meet hate with love, physical force with soul force." He urged the assembled protestants to go back to their states and to their communities with new determination, remembering always that things would be difficult and that they would be sorely tried. "It is always difficult," he said to a fervent counterpoint of "amens," "to get out of Egypt."

After the Prayer Pilgrimage, a great many Americans were convinced that King was the man to lead the way. James L. Hicks, editor of the *New York Amsterdam News*, said King had "emerged from the Prayer Pilgrimage to Washington as the number one leader of sixteen million Negroes in the United States. . . . At this point in his career, the people will follow him anywhere." Hicks and other journalists and a great many average citizens persisted, to King's chagrin, in comparing him with Roy Wilkins, usually to the disadvantage of the latter. There followed a series of articles alleging a "feud" between Wilkins and the new leader. King issued frequent denials and said his approach was "a supplement," not "a substitute" for the law-oriented NAACP approach. Despite denials, the rumors spread. King finally flew to New York City and ostentatiously took out a life membership in the NAACP. Still, the rumors persisted, fueled not only by man's ancient desire to see other people fighting, but also by deepening disillusionment with the traditional approaches of Negro leadership.

The Negro leadership spectrum just then was in a state of considerable confusion, and the energies released by King and Montgomery intensified the strain. As King's star rose, voices within and without the National Urban League and the NAACP called for a new departure and a re-examination of basic premises. Militants within the league formed an *ad hoc* committee, the "Disturbed Committee of the Executive Secretaries Council," to fight for a more daring program. Edwin C. (Bill) Berry, who later became executive secretary of the Chicago Urban League, was chairman of the committee which contended that the league had "played it so safe that we are well behind the safety zone."

"This is the last half of the twentieth century," Berry said later in an address to the league, "the age of sputniks as well as the age of urban sprawl. Negroes have emerged from two and one-half world wars, with a new dimension of personal significance. They are no longer willing to be half-slave and half-free. They are at war with the status quo, and will no longer accept the leadership of any agency or organization that does not know this and will not act on it forthrightly. People who do not mean business do not walk with Martin Luther King or stand with Daisy Bates. . . . Uncle Tom's day is over and Uncle Thomas' days are numbered. (Uncle Thomas is an Uncle Tom with a college degree and a Brooks Brothers suit.)"

The NAACP was undergoing a similar crisis of purpose. Walter White, the longtime secretary, had died in 1955 and had been succeeded by Roy Wilkins, a former newspaper editor (*Kansas City Call*), who joined the organization in 1931. It would be Wilkins' fate to preside over the NAACP in one of the most turbulent periods in its history. He was no sooner settled in his seat than the specter of King appeared on the horizon. Then, in triphammer blows, came the rout of litigation in the South and a wave of lynchings and bombings. Finally, and most ominously, the South began in 1956 to strike at the roots of the organization, filing suits against Negro lawyers for "soliciting" civil rights cases and harassing state organizations by subpoenaing their membership lists.

To make things even more vexing for the Negro leadership class, which was organized around the NAACP and Urban League approaches, Negro activists chose this moment to question its basic postulates. The South and a surprisingly large number of white liberals said the NAACP was going too fast, but voices in the ghetto said the organization was going too slow. James Hicks, the New York editor, said in a celebrated article that neither Walter White nor his successor, Roy Wilkins, was a "true" Negro leader. Hicks charged that Wilkins was a "captive" of prominent whites on the NAACP board. Jackie Robinson, a member of the board, did not endorse Hicks' views, but he declared in no uncertain terms that the organization was not reaching the "little man." He was particularly disturbed, according to a 1958 interview, about "the failure on the part of the organization" to do an effective selling job. What Jackie Robinson and others called for was a more "aggressive" posture.

In the eye of the storm, buffeted by critics of the left and right, sat Roy Wilkins, who was born in 1901 and was graduated from the University of Minnesota in 1923. Tall, thin, tactically astute, Wilkins was extremely able in the area he marked off for himself: administrative expertise and lobbying. He had come up through the NAACP bureaucracy and was, accordingly, a desk-oriented man who lacked King's charisma and personal magnetism.

What was the new secretary's program?

Wilkins' program was the NAACP's/program and that program had not changed, really, since the days of King's grandfather. Negro interests, he believed, were best served by tactics of litigation and lobbying. He did not then, nor does he now, believe in the use of combat tactics (demonstrations, picketing, boycotting) as a primary tactic of struggle.

It looks simpler now than it did then. With the aid of hindsight, we can see clearly that events were foreclosing the possibilities of the dominant Negro leadership styles. The grain of history was moving in King's direction and the Negro leadership class, Wilkins included, would have to move with the grain or lose the power to make and shape events.

They are deluded who say the despairing rebel. Men have to drink deep draughts of hope before they will throw themselves against the walls of their cage. It was King's achievement to give men hope—that and the second indispensable element of a revolt, a new idea. King's significance in this his first period of national leadership lay primarily in the direction and momentum he gave to the diffuse gropings of the people. In this season, a deep groundswell of anticipation surged through the Negro masses and, pushing upward, met the revolutionary ideas King was shooting downward. By giving the people another ideology, old and yet new, alien and yet indigenous, King gave them a new way of thinking about their condition and a new tool for changing it. Above everything else, King sensed and managed to convey to articulate strata in the Negro community, particularly youth, the revolutionary idea that the explosive force needed for the freeing of Negroes had to be generated within the breasts of Negroes. In the years between 1957 and 1960, King's time was spent essentially in two exercises: 1) the staking out of a claim to a new posture, and 2) the slow striving to catch the eyes and the ears of the populace. Though far from clear about either his means or his end, King nevertheless played an immensely important role as a sower of seeds of discontent.

Paradoxically, King's main thrust in this period was political. Following his political-oriented plea at the Prayer Pilgrimage, he attempted to organize a "Crusade for Citizenship." Although the SCLC-backed "crusade" included "education and action," the heart of the matter was a drive to register five million new Negro voters in the South. As late as December, 1959, King and SCLC, with NAACP support and help, were involved in attempts to increase the number of registered voters in the South.

Deeply distressed by the increasing militancy of the white resistance movement, King redoubled his efforts to involve the federal government in the Negro struggle. In speeches, interviews, and articles, he hammered away at the theme of government responsibility. In a two-hour conference with Vice-President Richard Nixon on June 13, 1957, he pleaded for executive leadership in what was fast becoming a major domestic problem. King was accompanied to the Washington conference by Ralph D. Abernathy. Both men sought assurances that the President or Vice-President would come to the South to make a major speech on civil rights as a moral as well as a legal problem. King considered the Little Rock integration crisis which flared soon afterward as a logical result of the dilatory tactics of the federal government. Asking again for a conference with President Eisenhower, King said that "Little Rock points a dramatic finger to the urgent necessity for the President to confer with Negro leaders from across the country." On King's initiative, a White House conference was arranged. The conference, which was held on June 23, 1958, was also attended by Randolph, Wilkins, and Lester B. Granger, then executive director of the Urban League. By prearrangement, Randolph served as spokesman for the group, reading a nine-point proposal agreed upon by the four most eminent Negro leaders.

1. The President of the United States, should declare in a nationwide pronouncement, prior to September, that the law will be vigorously upheld with the total resources at his command.

2. Much emphasis has been laid on the need for restoring communication between white and colored Southerners who are troubled by a common fear of reaction. The President can well set the example in this matter by convoking a White House Conference of constructive leadership to discuss ways and means of complying peaceably with the Court's rulings.

3. Information, resources, and advice of the appropriate government agencies addressed to the problems of integration should be made available to all officials and community groups seeking to work out a program of education and action.

4. The President should request both parties to lay aside partisanship so that the Congress can enact a civil rights bill which will include Part III originally in the 1957 bill, in order that constitutional rights other than voting rights may be enforced by the United States Attorney General. Lack of adequate and clear statutory authority has made the Federal government a mere spectator in the disgraceful maneuverings at Little Rock.

5. We urge the President to direct the Department of Justice to give all legal assistance possible under the law, including both the filing of a brief as a friend of the court and appearance of counsel, in the appeal from the [Judge Harry] Lemley decision in the Little Rock case.

6. The President of the United States should direct the Department of Justice to act now to protect the right of citizens to register and vote. In the nine months since the enactment of the 1957 Civil Rights Act, overt acts have been committed against prospective Negro registrants in some areas and numerous complaints have been submitted to the Department, but to date, not a single case has reached a court of law. Unless immediate action is undertaken, thousands of Negro citizens will be denied the right to cast a ballot in the 1958 elections.

7. The President should direct the Department of Justice to act under existing statutes in the wave of bombings of churches, synagogues, homes and community centers; also in the murderous brutality directed against Negro citizens in Dawson, Georgia, and other communities.

8. In order to counteract the deliberate hamstringing of the new Civil Rights Commission, the President should recommend to the Congress the extension of its life for at least a full year beyond its present expiration date.

9. The President should make it clear both in statement and in act that he believes in the principle that federal money should not be used to underwrite segregation in violation of the federal constitutional rights of millions of Negro citizens, and that this principle should be applied whether in matters of federal aid to education, hospitals, housing, or any other grants-in-aid to state and local government. In sup-

port of national policy, the Federal Government should finance continuation of public schools where state funds are withdrawn because of integration.

Such were the necessities of the moment as Martin Luther King, Jr., and other Negro leaders saw them and spoke of them to Dwight David Eisenhower in June of 1958. The President, in response, said little. He spoke of the harrowing complexity of the problem and of the need to change men's hearts, but he gave the Negro leaders little encouragement and they went away empty-handed to face the withering criticism of the Negro press. Eisenhower impressed King then as a good but insufficiently briefed man who knew little of the facts of Negro life. In fact, it seemed to King that the President was a little bewildered by the demands of the Presidency. At one point in the conference, with King at his side, President Eisenhower said: "Reverend, there are so many problems—Lebanon, Algeria. . . ."

From time to time, in 1957 and 1958, King made tentative forays into the field of direct action, suggesting, on one occasion, massive stand-ins in Southern polling booths and, on another, study-ins in white Southern schools. The response to these proposals was cool, even hostile. Thurgood Marshall and other leaders said of the second proposal that it was neither wise nor heroic to send children to do the work of men. Crestfallen, King retreated, consoling himself perhaps with the idea that the time was not yet ripe. King did not reply to his critics. But he later spoke with unusual—for him—severity of the difficulties of a social prophet. "A methodology and philosophy of revolution," he wrote in *Why We Can't Wait*, "is neither born nor accepted overnight. From the moment it emerges, it is subjected to rigorous tests, opposition, scorn and prejudice. The old guard in any society resent new methods, for old guards wear the decorations and medals won by waging battle in the accepted manner. . . ." While awaiting the maturation of events, King busied himself with what was essentially a ministry of interpretation. Two or three times a week, sometimes more often, he flew in and out of the Montgomery airports, winging his way to cities north, south, east, and west, spreading the message of the coming of the new day.

Galley proof of first book, Stride Toward
Freedom, is discussed by author and Cass
Canfield, chairman of executive com-
mittee of Harper & Row.

Stabbed in chest (arrow) by demented
woman while autographing books in
Harlem department store, he awaits
arrival of ambulance. Assailant was
committed to insane asylum.

At Harlem Hospital, King is examined by Dr. Emil Naclerio, who helped remove steel letter opener in delicate, three-hour operation. Dr. Naclerio said King was "a sneeze away from death." King said assassination attempt was a product of a climate of hatred. He was released from hospital on October 3, 1958.

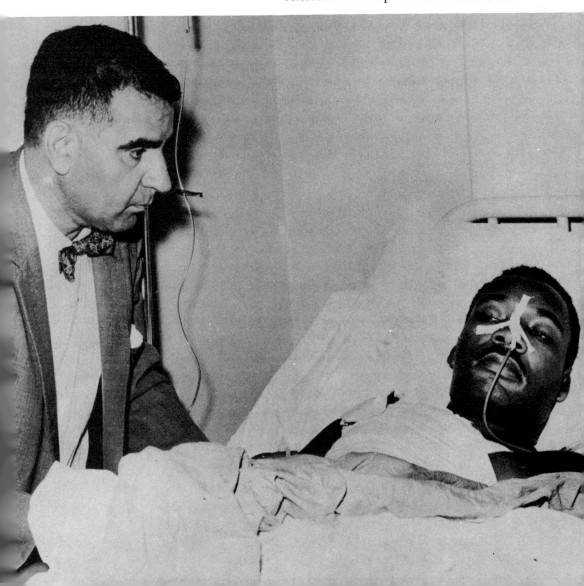

An extension of this ministry of interpretation and of King's education was his 1957 trip to Ghana as an official government guest at the independence celebration of the first African colony to win its freedom. To King and Coretta, the Ghana celebration was a deep, almost mystical experience. To walk on the ground from which came hundreds of years before the mysterious forebears no one could name and no one could forget; to walk the streets of a land where color no longer mattered; to see black policemen, black judges, black ministers, and to dine with a black prime minister; to sit finally in the huge darkened stadium and to watch the black man's flag rise in a new setting: these were horizon-shattering experiences that pulled them out of themselves toward their goals. King said later that the Ghana trip was one of the most meaningful experiences of his life.

Refreshed physically and spiritually, despite a bout of illness in Ghana, King returned to America with a new sense of purpose and a new faith in the ultimate triumph of his cause. During the rest of the year, he was in almost perpetual motion. His activities of this period can be gauged by a *Jet* magazine feature, "Man on the Go," which said that King delivered 208 speeches that year and traveled 780,000 miles. By secreting himself in the homes of Montgomery friends and in an Atlanta hotel he completed his first book, an autobiographical account of the Montgomery struggle called *Stride Toward Freedom*.

If there was a ministry of interpretation, there was also a ministry of pain. King's third arrest on Wednesday, September 3, marked the beginning of a period of tribulation. The arrest grew out of a court hearing involving King's friend, Ralph D. Abernathy. King and Coretta and a group of friends and admirers were standing outside the Montgomery Recorder's Court when an officer ordered the group to move. What happened next is a matter of controversy. The officer said King refused to obey the order. King said that he asked to see Attorney Fred D. Gray and was told: "If you don't get the 'so-and-so' out of here, you'll need a lawyer." At that point, witnesses said, two officers grabbed King, saying: "Boy, you done done it now." The officers put a "hammerlock" on King, pushed him down the stairs and through the streets to the nearby jail. Coretta King, tearful and "in great distress," followed the procession. She said the officers waved her away, shouting: "You want to go, too, gal? Just nod your head." King told her, quickly: "Don't say anything, darling."

At the jail, King was searched and then "pushed and kicked," he said, into a cell. He was booked on a charge of loitering (later changed to disobeying an officer) and released on bond. In the wake of this event, King made a momentous stride toward Gandhi. When he reached his house that day, he told the assembled friends and aides, "I've had enough of this thing." After a day of "prayerful consideration" and a long talk with Coretta, he decided to go to jail instead of paying the fine. The germ of this decision had been stirring in King for a long time. As a result of reading and meditation, he had come to a deeper understanding of the demands of Gandhism. Two weeks before this incident, a group of Indians had spent part of three days with the Kings. After this visit, Coretta said later, "we began to think more deeply about the whole philosophy of nonviolence. We talked about how superficial and shallow our knowledge of the whole thing was." To Coretta as well as to King, the arrest seemed to be one chain in a whole link of events leading to a deeper commitment to the cause of passive resistance and freedom.

True to his word, King opted to go to jail. Nothing indicates more clearly the height to which he had then come than the fact that the police commissioner hastily paid his fine. In an extraordinary statement, Commissioner Clyde C. Sellers said he could not permit King "to use the facilities of the City of Montgomery for his own selfish purposes." Sellers charged darkly that King had engineered the whole thing as a "publicity stunt" and said that he (Sellers) had "elected to spare the taxpayers of Montgomery the expense of feeding and housing him during the next fourteen days." King protested, but the whole of Montgomery officialdom seemed united now in a determination to keep him out of jail.

After the trial, a large crowd of Montgomery Negroes marched to Dexter Avenue Baptist Church for a protest meeting which became a victory celebration on the unexpected release of King. King himself made a dramatic entrance at 1:43 P.M. As he marched up the aisle, men and women reached out to touch him and to shake his hands. King brought the crowd to its feet by announcing immediately that he would never again pay a fine in court for any charge stemming "from our fight for freedom." "If I am convicted of a charge of that nature, I will refuse to pay the fine." Then, as the applause died down, King said: "I told the judge to either declare me innocent or let me serve my *time.*

fine. But when the white people of Montgomery saw that Martin Luther King wasn't afraid to go to jail they couldn't stand up with the courage to put me in jail." King then repeated what was by now a ritual argument, imploring his followers to refrain from violence and to "meet physical force with soul force." "Blood," he said, "may flow in the streets of Montgomery before we receive our freedom, but it must be our blood that flows and not that of the white man. We must not harm a single hair on the head of our white brothers." He saw a brighter future ahead. "Some day—it may be a year, ten years or even longer— but some day all the people of Montgomery are going to live together as brothers. There may be some delays, but one day we shall all live on an integrated basis." He was happy to suffer for that future. "When I go to jail, the whole world knows it. I have hundreds of telegrams and I have received telephone calls from nearly every state in the union. But when one of you go to jail and suffer brutality, no one knows about it. I am happy that I could suffer just a little bit. I am happy that I could suffer a little of what Jimmy Wilson is suffering for being convicted of robbery of less than two dollars. I am happy to suffer a little. . . . It makes me feel a closer part of you."

Turning now to the future, King said: "We have a mandate from God to resist evil. . . . We must go out of this meeting with a determination to take a firm and courageous stand against police brutality. We must go out and no longer be afraid to go to jail. This has taught us one thing, that we no longer have to fear going to jail."

The harshness of this episode was softened by the excellent reviews King received on the publication of his first book on September 17. Under terms of his contract, he was required to make public appearances in several Northern cities. The crowds were large and receptive in Detroit and even larger in Chicago. In Harlem, however, on Friday night, September 19, King was heckled by black nationalists who took exception to his doctrine of love and to his scheduled appearance at Blumstein's, a white-owned store in the heart of Harlem. When King arrived at Blumstein's the next day, he took a seat at an improvised desk in the shoe section of the department store and began to autograph books. He paid no particular attention to a heavy-set woman, gold earrings dangling, who pushed her way through the crowd and asked a store employee: "Is this Martin Luther King?" The employee said: "Yes, it is." The woman pushed her way to King and asked: "Are you Mr. King?" King nodded: "Yes, I am." The woman cursed, pulling at the same time a Japanese letter opener from the front of her dress. "Luther King," she said, "I have been after you for five years." With that, she brought her hand down as hard as she could, driving the steel letter opener into the upper left side of King's chest. She then rained blows on King, babbling incoherently. Pulled away, the woman dashed for the door but was subdued by onlookers who held her for the police. The store by now was a dervish of screaming, hysterical women, one of whom almost ended King's life instantly by trying to pull the letter opener from his chest. Fortunately, a man interceded and King, still conscious and calm, was rushed to Harlem Hospital with the letter opener still in his chest.

Meanwhile, policemen were questioning his assailant, Mrs. Izola Ware Curry, a forty-two-year-old woman who had lived in New York on and off for half of her life. In her dress, police found a second weapon, a small Italian automatic. Izola Curry, clearly deranged, gave several incoherent versions of her motives. She said at one point that "people were torturing me." She also accused King, whom she had never seen before, of trying to convert her from Roman Catholicism. To policemen and reporters at the West 123rd Street station, the domestic worker rambled, identifying herself as an anti-integrationist who wanted to kill King because he was "head of the NAACP."

In the wake of the attempted assassination, rumors blanketed Harlem. That day and for several days afterward Harlemites were convinced that the stabbing was a part of an organized conspiracy by either black nationalists or white supremacists. It was therefore a highly inflamed crowd which gathered before Harlem Hospital, where Dr. Aubré Maynard and a team of surgeons were removing the letter opener from King's chest. (To reach the wound, the surgeons had to remove part of one rib.) After the operation which took almost three hours, King was placed on the critical list. Only his wife, who flew to New York from Montgomery, and other members of the family were allowed to see him. Dr. Emil A. Naclerio, one of the three surgeons who performed the operation, said later that the sharp tip of the blade had penetrated to the outer wall of the aorta, the main arterial trunk that pipes blood from the heart to other parts of the body. "He was just a sneeze away from death," he said, adding: "Had he sneezed or coughed, the weapon would have penetrated the aorta."

Izola Curry was arraigned the next day before Magistrate Vincent Rao. The bespectacled woman stood before the bench, defiant, her arms crossed.

"I understand," the magistrate said, "this is the woman accused of stabbing the Rev. Mr. King with a knife." Izola Curry corrected him.

"No, it was a letter opener."

Assistant District Attorney Howard Jones said quickly: "I would like her held without bail."

Again, Mrs. Curry interrupted.

"I'm charging him as well as he's charging me."

"What have you got against him?" Magistrate Rao asked.

"I'm charging him with being mixed up with communists. I've reported the case to the FBI and it's being looked into. . . . "

"This woman is ill," Magistrate Rao said.

Over her objections, Mrs. Curry was committed to Bellevue Hospital Psychiatric Ward for mental examination. She was later committed to the Mattewan State Hospital for the Criminally Insane.

King, meanwhile, was mending, despite a "slight touch" of pneumonia. Messages and flowers poured into the hospital from all parts of the world. Governor Averell Harriman came to call. Vice-President Nixon sent a message; so also did religious and labor groups, interracial ministerial alliances in the North and South, the crew of the SS America, and a group of Los Angeles redcaps. King was buoyed up by this national outpouring of love and affection, but he told Coretta, with a chuckle, that some of the messages committing him prematurely to the heavens beyond "were kind of gloomy." During the convalescence period, Coretta served as a buffer between King and VIPs who visited the hospital. The hospital thoughtfully provided an office and Coretta spent most of the day commuting between King's tenth-floor room and the first floor. Intrigued by his wife's activities, King said finally: "I don't understand why there is so much *business* around my getting sick." What King could not understand was the fact that his brush with death underlined: he had become an American institution whose goings, comings, and jailings would hereafter be a matter of national moment.

King's attitude toward his assailant was consistent with his approach to life. In his first hospital press conference, King said he felt "no ill will toward Mrs. Izola Curry" and that he hoped "all thoughtful people will do all in their power to see that she gets the help she apparently needs if she is to become a free and constructive member of society." Seated in a wheelchair, flanked by relatives and close friends, King went on to make a remarkable prediction which pointed to the assassinations of 1963. "The pathetic aspect of this experience," he said on Tuesday, September 30, 1958, "is not the injury to one individual. It demonstrates that a climate of hatred and bitterness so permeates areas of our nation that inevitably deeds of extreme violence must erupt. Today it was I. Tomorrow it could be another leader or any man, woman or child who will be the victim of lawlessness and brutality."

Three days later, King was released from the hospital. (Though declared "completely cured," he and the doctors realized that the nature of the wound and the steps necessary to reach it pointed to the fact that he would probably suffer slight repercussions as long as he lived.)

After a brief convalescence in New York, he left for Montgomery to re-enter the struggle. After resting there for several weeks, he turned his mind to one of the great dreams of his life, a trip to India. He had a long-standing invitation from Prime Minister Nehru, but had never been able to work it into his schedule. Now, with his desk relatively clear and a grant from SCLC and the American Friends Service Committee, he made preparations for his second trip abroad. Accompanied by Coretta and a close friend, Lawrence D. Reddick, he left America in early February and arrived in New Delhi on February 10. To the delight of the Indians, most of whom were familiar with his work, he said: "To other countries I may go as a tourist, but to India, I come as a pilgrim." From New Delhi, King traveled across the country, holding frequent press conferences and speaking at universities and colleges. He also made the traditional pilgrimage to Gandhi's shrine at New Delhi.

King was struck by signs of great suffering and poverty and he marveled over the deep spirituality of the Indian people, a legacy, he said, of the Gandhian struggle. Most of all, he was impressed by Gandhi's living monument, Jawaharlal Nehru. The Kings and Reddick dined with Nehru and conferred with him at great length. Nehru, an aristocratic Brahman who had gone to jail several times during the Gandhian struggle, seemed so different from the politicians King had known. An elegant blending of the man of action and the man of ideas, Nehru was committed not to the "art of the possible" but to

Harlem banner advertises "Prayer Pilgrimage" Which King helped to organize. Other leaders were Roy Wilkins of NAACP and labor leader Asa Philip Randolph.

Man of the hour, King holds crowd spellbound with impassioned plea for political rights. "Give us the ballot!" he shouted six times and the crowd chanted the words after him. He received standing ovation before and after speech.

Huge crowd, which came from thirty states, heard twelve speeches and four prayers. Pilgrimage was designed to prod the nation's conscience on the issues of school desegregation and voting rights. It marked emergence of King as national leader, and was also an unprecedented alliance of the NAACP, labor, and the Negro church.

broad ends involving the destiny of man. Nehru, moreover—and this impressed King greatly—had a large vision of the responsibility of his government to take affirmative action in improving the lot of the untouchables. On three occasions in three weeks, King heard Nehru make speeches condemning untouchability and he could not help thinking how different was the case in America, where the President was silent. To King's surprise, Nehru even endorsed the idea of national atonement, of special and intensive efforts to root out the effects of thousands of years of soul-destroying oppression. King wrote later: "When I talked with Nehru about that he said, we couldn't think of talking about refusing to discriminate against untouchables without thinking somehow of doing something ourselves and taking some responsibility to lift the standards of the people whom we have exploited all these years. He said that might be a little discrimination in reverse, giving them something we don't give others—but this, he said, was our way of atoning for what we have done to these people for thousands of years."

King returned to America convinced more than ever of the necessity of massive government intervention and of the efficacy of love, *Satygraha*, and suffering in forcing a government to that step. But there was no evidence in the land to which he returned in 1959 that the meek and humble would inherit the earth. Across the South there was a wave of bombings and atrocities capped by the April 25 lynching of Mack James Parker in Poplarville, Mississippi. More ominous yet was the open defiance of the Civil Rights Commission and other federal agencies by Deep South segregationists.

If the sap of Southerners was rising, the wrath of Negroes was also nearing an explosion point. Symptomatic of the general unrest was the growing influence of Elijah Muhammad's black nationalist movement which repudiated love and passive resistance and called for the establishment of a black state in some unspecified place. Even more significant, though no one remarked it at the time, was the restiveness of Negro youth. As early as August, 1958, NAACP Youth Councils in Wichita, Kansas, and Oklahoma City had exploded in a series of sit-ins. And in both 1958 and 1959 Negro youth had staged mass marches on Washington to protest the slow pace of desegregation. Now, in the fall of 1959, the social seismographs were swinging wildly and before long somebody was going to have to do something.

And what was King doing all this time?

He was waiting and watching, listening with ever-increasing excitement to an internal radar that told him that it was time to move. For some time now, King had been struggling with a decision. He liked Montgomery, felt that he owed Montgomery something. Yet he could not shake the feeling that he could make a larger contribution from another base, from Atlanta perhaps, where a copastorship with his father would free him of the details of the pastoral round. Finally, after great thought and some prodding by the executive board of SCLC, King made the "painful decision" to resign and return to Atlanta. There remained only the delicate task of informing the members of his church. Though King had told only his trustees and a few intimates, word leaked out, and on Sunday, November 29, 1959, Dexter Avenue Baptist Church was filled. Reporters who covered the occasion said everyone seemed tense. King sat in the pulpit, looking uncomfortable and preoccupied. Behind him in the choir Coretta sat with the sopranos, giving no hint of anything amiss.

Tension thickened when King rose to give the sermon. King talked for a moment or two about that "flux in the universe" and the fact that only change itself did not change. The crowd waited, impatiently. This was no day for Hegel; this was a day for a man to speak only of visions he himself had seen. King must have sensed that for he began now to talk of the critical events "of the last few days." He spoke of his inability to relax enough to compose his sermon for that day. He hadn't been able "to think like I should have" and he believed it would be an "imposition to attempt to preach when I am not prepared to do it." Unexpectedly, he turned the pulpit over to the Rev. T. E. Brooks, who spoke for twenty minutes. Before delivering the benediction, King asked the members to remain for a brief business meeting. When the church was clear of all except church members, King again approached the pulpit. "What I want to say," he began, "I know you are already aware of. News has a way of traveling. I chose this time to say it because we are coming to the end of our church year, and I have a moral obligation to let you know what my plans are."

King leaned now to the side of the pulpit, clutching it for support.

"For almost four years now," he continued, "I have been faced with the responsibility of trying to do as one man what five or six people ought to be doing. This all began because of the injustices which we faced on the buses. I found myself in a position I could not get out of. This thrust unexpected responsibilities my way." With obvious weariness, King named his pastorate, the presidency of SCLC, the presidency of the Montgomery Improvement Association, extensive speaking engagements, day-to-day office chores, and *"the general strain of being known"* as the chief reasons for a "great internal frustration." He said he feared losing his "creative" freshness. "What I have been doing is giving, giving, *giving*, and not stopping to retreat and meditate like I should—to come back. If the situation is not changed, I will be a physical and psychological wreck. I have to reorganize my personality and reorient my life. I have been too long in the crowd, too long in the forest. . . ."

King digressed for a moment, dispersing the accumulating tension. Then he said: "I can't stop now. History has thrust something upon me which I cannot turn away. *I should free you now.*" King paused for a long moment and said:

"I would like to submit my resignation as pastor of Dexter Avenue Baptist Church to become effective on the fourth Sunday in January."

With reluctance, with foreboding, with scattered muttering, the resignation was accepted by all except eleven elderly women and an old man who voted "no" to show that "we weren't just going to give him up without some kind of fight." The voting over, the regrets said, King asked everyone to link hands and join him in the song, "Blest Be the Tie That Binds." As the melody rose and fell, Martin Luther King, Jr., broke down in tears in the pulpit that had carried him to fame.

Symbol

I т is a great art, possibly the greatest art, to know when to move, when to break roots, often in pain and tears, when to shake hands and say goodbye, when to shake old soil off growing feet and strike out, not looking back, for the new. It is, as I say, a great art to know when to do this—and Martin Luther King, Jr., seemed to know it.

Let us look closely at this young man as he stood in January, 1960, on the edge of an approaching storm. For three years, for thirty-six months, he had *done* nothing, except sow seeds. Now suddenly he was seized by an urge to roam, convinced that the harvest was near. How explain this? It was, of course, unexplainable, even to King. Though unexplainable, it was nevertheless highly significant, another relevant factor indicating King's predestined relation to his times. Though King *knew* more then than he could explain, though he was as surprised as the next man by the advent of the sit-in age, his formal statement on the reasons for his impending move to Atlanta was certainly one of the most significant in the history of Negro leadership.

For in this statement, dated December 1, 1959, King announced boldly that the proper "psychological moment" had come. "The time has come," he announced, "for a broad, bold advance of the Southern campaign for equality. After prayerful consideration, I am convinced that *the psychological moment has come when a concentrated drive against injustice can bring great tangible gains. We must not let the present strategic opportunity pass.* Very soon our new program will be announced. Not only will it include a stepped-up campaign of voter registration, but a full-scale assault will be made upon discrimination and segregation in all forms. *We must train our youth and adult leaders in the techniques of social change through nonviolent resistance. We must employ new methods of struggle, involving the masses of the people.*" [Emphasis supplied.]

While King was moving to his new charge to take advantage of the proper "psychological moment," the Bastille of the Negro Revolution began to fall. On Thursday, February 1, at 4:45 in the afternoon, four Negro students sat down at a lunch counter in Greensboro, North Carolina. Eight days later, the sit-in technique spread to Charlotte. Sixteen days later it leaped the bounds of North Carolina and began to race across the South. By the end of March, sit-ins had been staged at lunch counters, department stores, supermarkets, theaters, and libraries in cities in every state of the South except Mississippi. By that time, too, the basic sit-in technique (taking a seat in a white facility and refusing to move when ordered or to fight back when attacked) was being supplemented by stand-ins, kneel-ins, and mass marches in downtown areas.

The sit-ins, as King realized almost immediately, were the real turning point in race relations in America. Montgomery had been a stride toward rebellion; Greensboro and the cities beyond were rebellion itself. As the rebellion raced across the land, King watched, fascinated, recognizing in it the fruit of his own efforts and the fruit of his dream.

The sit-in movement, by all accounts, was a spontaneous development with deep roots in the germinal events of the late fifties. Almost without exception, the young student rebels said they were motivated by a deep dissatisfaction with the pace of desegregation and something approaching disgust with the traditional tactics of the Negro leadership class. Most of the student rebels recalled Montgomery and King as the central event and dominant image of their formative years.

King's germinative influence on the sit-in generation was underlined in a psychosocial study, "Youth and Social Action: Nonviolence in the South," by Dr. Frederic Solomon and Dr. Jacob R. Fishman. "[The Montgomery boycott] occurred," they wrote, "when many of these students were about fifteen years old, two years after they heard the Supreme Court tell them that their anger against segregation was justified and sanctioned. Young people all over the South were greatly impressed with the Montgomery boycott. They felt it was a lesson in the practical and emotional 'advantages of direct action' in expressing legitimate Negro discontent. Martin Luther King became the image of an assertive male assuming freedom of action with dignity and achieving respectful recognition through successful struggle with the white community (i.e., male community). In a sense he became the figure that the Negro adolescents wished their fathers might have been and as such became incorporated as part of their ego-ideals. Three years later, soon after leaving home for college, they would be acting on the dictates of this new identification model through the sit-in. . . ."

The sit-in age, which King's image helped to create, created a new King with a new mandate and a new mission. Recognized by almost everyone as the "spiritual father" of the sit-in students, King stepped forward immediately as a spokesman and symbol of the movement. King and his organization also made more tangible contributions. SCLC affiliates in Nashville, Tallahassee, and Montgomery played pivotal roles in pushing the movement forward, as did units of CORE which emerged now as a major civil rights organization.

King's major contribution, however, was in the structuring of student discontent. As King knew, reform movements in the Negro community were usually characterized by what physicists call low specific heat. They tended, in other words, to take flame quickly and to die out quickly. As the weeks wore on, King became increasingly concerned over the distinct possibility that the initial burst of energy would dissipate for lack of a structure. King and SCLC aides, particularly Ella Baker, decided, therefore, to organize a Southwide conference of sit-in student leaders. Some two hundred Negro college students representing forty communities in ten states attended the meeting on April 15-17 on the campus of Shaw University in Raleigh, North Carolina. In his keynote address, King stressed the need to "evolve a strategy of victory" and to develop: 1) "some type of continuing organization," 2) "a nationwide campaign of selective buying," and 3) "a group of volunteers who will willingly go to jail rather than pay bail or fines." It seemed to King also that the student leaders should "delve deeper into the philosophy of nonviolence. It must be made palpably clear that resistance and nonviolence are not in themselves good. There is another element in our struggle that then makes our resistance and nonviolence truly meaningful. That element is reconciliation. Our ultimate end must be the creation of the beloved community. The tactics of nonviolence without the spirit of nonviolence may become a new kind of violence."

King touched here on a matter of extreme delicacy. Although the students honored King as a nonviolent pioneer, some of them did not think he was radical enough and many accepted nonviolence as Nehru accepted it, as a tactic "promising certain results" and not "as a religion or an unchallengeable creed or dogma." It seemed to Helen Fuller of the New Republic and to other observers that King's aide, James M. Lawson, a young Methodist minister, struck a deeper chord by dwelling "more on nonviolence as a political weapon." Helen Fuller wrote: "Where King is insistent on speaking in moral terms—actually changing the hearts of white and black segregationists—Lawson talks knowledgeably of 'power structures'. . . . To a question about biracial committees, Lawson's answer, mildly, was that they were a waste of time."

Out of this conference came the Student Nonviolent Coordinating Committee, a coordinating structure of student ferment organized around the tougher, more polemical Nehru posture Lawson articulated. This development and the mushroom growth of CORE, a Northern-based organization which also placed more stress on nonviolent action than on love, subtly threatened King's leadership posture. To make things even more complicated, King was embroiled at this moment in a legal suit that threatened to end or at least cripple his usefulness as a missionary of change. On Wednesday, February 17, in the midst of the spreading sit-in controversy, King was arrested at his Atlanta church office on an Alabama warrant. Two Fulton County sheriff's deputies made the arrest at the request of Alabama officials who said King had been indicted by the Montgomery County Grand Jury on two counts of perjury in the filing of his 1956 and 1958 state income tax returns. King, accompanied by his father, was arraigned before Fulton Superior Court Judge Jeptha Tanksley and released under

$2,000 bond. King professed astonishment at the charges, saying he had "no pretense to absolute goodness," but if he had "one virtue, it's honesty." The indictments, he said, were "another attempt by the state of Alabama to harass me because of the position I've taken in the civil rights struggle."

King was outwardly calm, but inside he churned with agitation. A sense of shame overwhelmed him. He was prepared for jail, mayhem, even death, anything and everything except this. To be accused before the world of enriching himself and using his people—and lying about it: this was a blow for which he was not prepared. It was not true, of course. "But who," he asked, "will believe me?" It seemed to him that he could detect already the knowing smirks of the cynics, of the men and women who were always willing to believe the worst, to say, "There, I told you, he's just like all the rest." In shame, King cancelled a scheduled speaking engagement in Chicago. How could he face them? How could he face anyone? For a long time, he walked up and down in his study. Then, of a sudden, it came to him that there were all kinds of crosses, all colors, all sizes, and that perhaps it required greater courage to face disgrace than to face death. King called the airport, made another reservation, and went to Chicago to stand before the people, head held high, as a man unjustly accused.

Having faced that trial, having looked into the face of another kind of evil, it was not difficult to face the trial itself. The case came on for a hearing in the new Montgomery courthouse. Sheriff's deputies, mounted on horseback, ringed the building to prevent "Negro demonstrations." The white horsemen were supported by five highway patrolmen who carried large clubs. King was defended by a team of able Negro lawyers, including Fred Gray of Montgomery, Hubert Delany of New York, and William Robert Ming of Chicago. The prosecution was led by an old King antagonist, Solicitor William Thetford.

King pleaded innocent to the charge of listing his 1956 income as $9,150 when, according to the state, it should have been $16,162, and reporting $25,248 in 1958 when the state contended that it was $45,-421. It quickly developed that the state's case rested on a very insecure foundation. King had told state income agents that they were making a "political audit" of his returns. Although he denied making "anywhere near" the amount of money they said he made, he paid the disputed amount "under strong pressure" before the indictment was returned.

As the trial progressed, King's attorneys succeeded in bringing out that the state had reached the higher figures by adding to King's personal income sums spent for transportation, hotels, and other expenses in connection with his extensive travels on behalf of civil rights. The case collapsed really on Thursday, May 26, when the state's star witness, Lloyd Hale, a state tax agent, admitted under cross-examination that he had found "no evidence of fraud" in the preparation of King's income tax return. Defense Attorney Ming drew from Hale the admission that he had told King that he (Hale) did not believe there was any fraud involved in the disputed returns. Hale also admitted making an error in computing the tax claimed by the state, finding it to be $1,722 when it should have been $1,667. Cross-examination by Ming further revealed that the check King wrote to cover the income tax claim had never been cashed. Hale said it was being held pending "a final determination of it." Ming pointedly asked how the state could bring perjury charges when the defendant's tax had not been determined. In his summation, Ming said the state resorted to "fraudulent techniques, in other words, a mathematical trick," in auditing King's returns. The state, Ming said, erroneously contended that "the taxpayer's gross income is the total of all the bank deposits he made in various banks in the year 1956."

The jury of twelve white men agreed. On Saturday, May 28, the white jury broke a Southern tradition and acquitted King after deliberating three hours and forty-five minutes. When the verdict was read, King betrayed no emotion. But Coretta and Defense Attorney Delany broke down in tears.

The next day, Sunday, May 29, King delivered a sermon entitled, "Autobiography of Suffering." To a welcoming throng which filled every seat in Ebenezer, King said there had been "no miraculous conversion" in Alabama but "something [had] happened to that jury." King then reviewed the past four years in the civil rights struggle and told how he had come to Atlanta from Montgomery "overjoyed by student demonstrations and determination." He said he had been bombed, jailed, shot at, but that the tax case had hit him hardest because "I was being attacked on honesty." In the audience that day was novelist James Baldwin, who detected "a new note of anguish" in King's voice. King spoke, or so it seemed to Baldwin, "more candidly than I had ever heard him speak before, of his bitterly assaulted pride, of his shame, when he found himself accused, before all the world, of having used and betrayed the people of Montgomery by stealing the money they had entrusted to him." It seemed to Baldwin that King had looked on "evil a long, hard, lonely time" and that he was beginning perhaps to understand that the Biblical injunction, "overcome evil with good," does not mean necessarily that good will *triumph* over evil.

Throughout 1961 and 1962, Martin Luther King, Jr., was a man in search of a mission. For most of this period, the headlines were dominated by other men and by children. Though not detached from the happenings of these years, King seemed somehow marginal. He flared up from time to time in great ventures and then disappeared from public view.

One of these flares, however, probably changed the course of American and human history. There was no hint at the beginning that the incident would become so weighty. On Wednesday, October 19, in the midst of the Presidential campaigns of Senator John F. Kennedy and Vice-President Richard Nixon, King and fifty-one other persons were arrested during a sit-in at Rich's department store. Through the good offices of Atlanta Mayor William Hartsfield the charges against the demonstrators were dropped and all except King were released. On order of Judge Oscar Mitchell, King was held for adjoining DeKalb County, where he had received a suspended twelve-month sentence on September 23 for driving without a Georgia driver's license. On Tuesday, October 25, King, in handcuffs, was taken from the Fulton County Jail to a DeKalb County court. There, over the strong objections of Attorney Donald L. Hollowell, Judge Mitchell ruled that King's participation in the sit-in had violated the terms of his twelve-month probated sentence. Judge Mitchell sentenced King to serve four months as a laborer in a state public works camp.

Before dawn the next morning, King was turned over to state board of correction officers. Four hours later, he was in the Reidsville State Prison in Tatnall County. By now, 8 P.M., Wednesday, word of the transfer was circling the globe, and wires were pouring into the office of Mayor William Hartsfield.

As King languished "in segregation"—a prison term for solitary confinement—his name began to exert a persuasive influence on America's most powerful men. That day, there was a high-level discussion at the Justice Department on what steps could be taken to free King. Several approaches were discussed, including filing a writ of habeas corpus in the federal courts and appearing as a friend of the court before Judge Mitchell. It was finally decided that the most effective approach would be a statement by President Eisenhower. The following statement was therefore drafted:

> It seems to me fundamentally unjust that a man who has peacefully attempted to establish his right to equal treatment, free from racial discrimination, should be imprisoned on an unrelated charge, in itself insignificant. Accordingly, I have asked the Attorney General to take all proper steps to join with Dr. Martin Luther King in an appropriate application for his release.

To the consternation of Negro Republicans, this statement was never issued. Worse, Vice-President Nixon chose to remain silent, saying he "would have no comment" on the jailing of the Negro leader.

Very different was the response in the Democratic camp. At that precise moment, the telephone line between Atlanta and Chicago, where John Kennedy was making a campaign stop, was alive with political speculation. The dominant figures in these conversations were Mayor Hartsfield and Attorney Morris B. Abrams of Atlanta and Harris Wofford, a Kennedy adviser on minority affairs. It was agreed finally that Kennedy should do or say something. Finally, after a long day of thinking and telephoning, Wofford came up with an idea that contained minimum political risk and the promise of maximum political advantage. Wofford passed the idea on to Sargent Shriver, Kennedy's brother-in-law, who reached Kennedy in Chicago. Kennedy considered the idea for a moment, crossed the room and was connected with King's wife. "Senator Kennedy said he was very much concerned about both of us," Coretta recalled. "He said this must be hard on me. He wanted me to know that he was thinking about us and he would do all he could to help. . . ." Questioned later about the call, John F. Kennedy said simply: "She is a friend of mine and I was concerned about the situation." Also concerned, it seems, was the Senator's brother and campaign manager, Robert F. Kennedy, who called Judge Mitchell "to inquire as to whether the Rev. Martin Luther King had a constitutional right to bail." The next day, Thursday, October 27, after deliberation and a review of King's appeal from the four-month prison term, Judge Mitchell decided that King had a right to bail, which was made immediately available. Attorney Hollowell rented an airplane and King was returned to Atlanta where a "thanksgiving prayer service" was held at Ebenezer Baptist Church. King told the meeting that he was deeply indebted to the Democratic Presidential candidate, but he stopped short of endorsing him. King's father had no such reservations. He announced during the meeting that he was switching his vote and support to Kennedy. "It took courage," he said, "to call my daughter-in-law at a time like this. Kennedy has the moral courage to stand up for what he knows is right." The story of the "two telephone calls" and Martin Luther King, Jr.'s expression of gratitude for the "humanitarian bent" of John F. Kennedy was widely publicized in the dying days of the campaign. Most students of the 1960 campaign believe the calls were primarily responsible for Kennedy's razor-thin edge over Richard Nixon. Ironically, Eisenhower would say later that "a couple of phone calls" had swung the Negro vote—and the election—to the Democrats.

After the inauguration of John Fitzgerald Kennedy, King redoubled his continuing efforts to involve the federal government in the deepening racial crisis. King saw in Kennedy "a leader unafraid of change," a young, bold, questing spirit. But he was deeply disturbed by Kennedy's initial vacillations. King would say later that "there were, in fact, two John Kennedys. One presided in the first two years under pressure of the uncertainty caused by his razor-thin margin of victory. He vacillated, trying to sense the direction his leadership could travel while retaining and building support for his Administration. However, in 1963, a new Kennedy had emerged. He had found that public opinion was not in a rigid mold. American political thought was not committed to conservatism, nor radicalism, nor moderation. It was above all fluid. As such it contained trends rather than hard lines, and affirmative leadership could guide it into constructive channels."

By repeated verbal thrusts and later by an act, Martin King shattered the "rigid mold" of public opinion and prepared the way for the emergence of the second Kennedy that the world will remember. Beginning with a *Nation* article, "Equality Now," King set out in early February to mobilize public opinion for a new departure by the federal government. "The new Administration," he wrote, "has the opportunity to be the first in one hundred years of American history to adopt a radically new approach to the question of civil rights." What did King suggest? "[The new Administration] must begin . . . with the firm conviction that the principle is no longer in doubt. The day is past for tolerating vicious and inhuman opposition on a subject which determines the lives of 20,000,000 Americans." Secondly, King said, there must be a "recognition by the federal government that it has sufficient power at its disposal to guide us through the changes ahead. The intolerably slow pace of civil rights is due at least as much to the limits which the federal government has imposed on its own actions as it is to the actions of the segregationist opposition."

In the following months, King intensified his pressure on the federal government, urging Kennedy to issue a Presidential executive order banning racial segregation in public facilities and to appoint a "Secretary of Integration." He also called for a Marshall Plan for America, a massive commitment of federal money and energy similar to the Alliance for Progress for South America. Such a plan, he said, should "define the specific steps to be taken by stages which will lift the nation into a new era. We are not strangers to such conceptions. The President has proposed a ten-year plan to put a man on the moon. We do not yet have a plan to put a Negro in the state legislature of Alabama."

"The development of a plan for the nation-wide and complete realization of civil rights," he continued, "would accomplish several purposes. It would affirm that the nation is committed to solve the problem within a stated period of time; it would establish that the full resources of government would be available to that end, whatever the cost. . . ."

By the end of the first year of the Kennedy Administration, King was openly denouncing the President for "critical indecisiveness." "It is not only that the Administration too often retreated in haste from a battlefield which it has proclaimed a field of honor," he wrote, "but— more significantly—its basic strategic goals have been narrowed. Its efforts have been directed toward limited accomplishments in a number of areas, affecting individuals and altering old patterns only superficially. Changes in depth and breadth are not yet in sight, nor has there been a commitment of resources adequate to enforce extensive change. It is a melancholy fact that the Administration is aggressively driving only toward the limited goal of token integration." Then, in his most acute analysis of social change, King said: "Many people of good will accept the achievement of steady advances, even when fractional. They feel simple addition must eventually accumulate a totality of social gains which will answer the problem. Others, however, viewing the task from the long perspective of history, are less sanguine. They are aware that the struggle being waged is against an opposition capable of the most tenacious resistance, either actively or through inertia. Such forces are not overcome by simple pressures, but only through constant exertion. . . .

"To illustrate, it is not practical to integrate buses, and then over an extended period of time expect to add another gain, and then another and another. Unfortunately, resistance stiffens after each limited victory; inertia sets in, and the forward movement not only slows down, but is often reversed entirely. What is required to maintain gains is an initial sweep of positive action so far-reaching that it immobilizes and weakens the adversary, thus depriving him of his power to retaliate. . . . In short, what is required is massive social mobilization uniting the strength of individuals, organizations, government, press and schools." King saw no evidence that the Kennedy Administration was prepared to mobilize the required social energy. His assessment of the first year of the New Frontier was harsh. "From this perspective, the New Frontier is unfortunately not new enough; and the Frontier is set too close to the rear."

King did not question the new President's sincerity; he questioned his sense of history. Meeting with Kennedy later, on October 16, 1962, King underlined his public contention that the "clock of history" was "nearing the midnight hour." In a one-hour conference at the White House, King urged Kennedy to issue a "second Emancipation Proclamation" declaring that racially segregated public facilities were "unconstitutional and illegal." Such a step, he said, was necessary to prevent Negro despair from rising "to an explosion point." Kennedy, a brilliant political being, deflected King's thrusts with parries. "With each new Negro protest," King wrote in *Why We Can't Wait*, "we were advised, sometimes privately and sometimes in public, to call off our efforts and channel all of our energies into registering voters. On each occasion we would agree with the importance of voting rights,

In India, the "Land of Gandhi," King addresses group of admirers. Young leader was accompanied by wife and friend, L. D. Reddick (r.), on February-March, 1959, trip.

Speaking to Indian group, King discusses Montgomery Bus Boycott and passive resistance. He discovered that details of Montgomery struggle were well known to the Indian people.

Prime Minister Jawaharlal Nehru, a Gandhi disciple, receives the Kings. Nehru expressed great interest in civil rights struggle. King also visited Gandhi's relatives.

Assisted by wife and Dr. Reddick, King places wreath on memorial tomb of Gandhi. King said he left India "more convinced than ever before that nonviolent resistance is the most potent weapon available" to oppressed people.

but would patiently seek to explain that Negroes did not want to neg-
lect all other rights while one was selected for concentrated attention."

Events in 1961-62—especially the Freedom Ride crisis—gave point
to King's growing concern over the seriousness of "the moral crisis."
King's role in the Freedom Rides was, like so many of his acts of that
period, peripheral and passive. The Freedom Rides, which were organized by CORE, were designed to dramatize the lack of compliance
with long-standing court orders and ICC rulings banning segregation
in interstate transportation. To emphasize this fact, thirteen Negroes
and whites left Washington on May 4, 1961, for an integrated bus ride
through the South. The trip was relatively uneventful in the Upper
South. Near Anniston, Alabama, however, on May 14, racists bombed
and burned the bus carrying the first group of Freedom Riders. Later
that day, the group was savagely assaulted in Birmingham. Since no
commercial bus would now transport them, the first group of Freedom
Riders abandoned the trip and flew to New Orleans. At this point a
second group of "Freedom Riders," organized by the militant student
cadre, picked up the baton. In Montgomery, on May 20, the new Freedom Riders were assaulted by another mob and Attorney General
Robert F. Kennedy rushed four hundred U.S. marshals to the city to
maintain public order. The next night, the Freedom Riders held a mass
meeting in the First Baptist Church of Montgomery. King, who had
rushed to the trouble spot, was the speaker of the hour. "The ultimate responsibility for the hideous action in Alabama last week must
be placed at the doorstep of the governor of the state," he said. "We
hear the familiar cry that morals cannot be legislated. This may be
true, but behavior can be regulated. The law may not be able to make
a man love me, but it can keep him from lynching me."

Lynching was precisely what the white mob gathered in front of the
First Baptist Church had in mind. The mob had been gathering for
hours. By nightfall, white segregationists controlled most of the area
in front of the Negro church. The only obstacles between the mob and
the one thousand Negroes inside the church were a squad of U.S. marshals and a handful of city policemen. "We want to integrate too,"
someone in the crowd yelled. Another voice said: "We'll get those niggers." A barrage of bottles and paving stones punctuated these words
and the marshals counterattacked with tear gas. As the battles raged
outside, King suggested that the Negro crowd inside the church link

hands and sing what was by now the *Marsellaise* of the Negro Revolution, "We Shall Overcome."

> The truth will make us free,
> The truth will make us free,
> The truth will make us free some day.
> Oh, deep in my heart, I do believe
> We shall overcome one day.

> We are not afraid,
> We are not afraid,
> We are not afraid today.
> Oh, deep in my heart, I do believe
> We shall overcome some day.

With Negroes singing freedom songs, with white Southerners and federal officials fighting in the streets of the capital of the old Confederacy, Governor John Patterson declared martial law and sent national guardsmen to the embattled church. The governor then called Attorney General Kennedy to inform him of his troop dispositions. The governor said pointedly, however, that Major General Henry Graham, the guard commander, could not guarantee the safety of Martin Luther King, Jr. "Have the general call me," Robert F. Kennedy snapped back. "I want him to say it to me. I want to hear a general of the U.S. Army say he can't protect Martin Luther King, Jr." Faced with an angry, determined attorney general, the Alabama governor retreated, admitting that it was he, not the general, who did not believe King could be protected.

Not only King but also the tattered nonviolent army of which he was the symbolic leader was protected. General Graham sealed off the church, dispersed the mob, and escorted King and the Negro crowd to their lodgings in the wee hours of the morning. In the following days, the organizations directly involved in the Freedom Rides—SCLC, CORE, SNCC—formed a Freedom Rider Coordinating Committee and named King spokesman. To prepare for the continuation of the campaign, the committee held nonviolent training sessions in the den of a fashionable three-story red-brick home in Montgomery. Among the leaders of these sessions were King, James Farmer of CORE, Diane Nash and Ed King of the Student Nonviolent Coordinating Committee, Ralph D. Abernathy, Wyatt Tee Walker and James Lawson of SCLC. At the final training session on Tuesday night, May 23, King listed the three main purposes of the rides: 1) "to test use of transportation facilities, according to federal law," 2) "to encourage others to demand use of the facilities," and 3) "to direct the spotlight of public attention to areas which still segregate." King added, his eyes searching out each of the rebels who would start the next morning for Mississippi: "Freedom Riders must develop the quiet courage of dying for a cause. We would not like to see anyone die. We all love life and there are no martyrs here—but we are well aware that we may have some casualties."

The following morning, reporters were alerted by a cryptic telephone message: "Seven comes eleven, the dogs don't run to Jackson." This meant that the riders would leave for Jackson, Mississippi, at 7 A.M. and 11 A.M. There have been few scenes in American history to compare with the assemblage that morning at the Montgomery bus terminal. Armed national guard troops lined both sides of the street in front of the terminal. Other troops, guns at the ready, surveyed the scene from the second level of a garage across the street. In faraway Washington, Robert F. Kennedy sat in his Justice Department office monitoring the arrangements on a special telephone device that enabled him to listen to local police radio messages. At 7 A.M., the first bus of twelve Freedom Riders, seventeen reporters and six armed soldiers pulled out of the Trailways bus terminal with an incredible escort of twenty-two highway patrol cars, two battalions of national guardsmen, three U.S. Army reconnaisance planes, and two helicopters. As the convoy headed for Jackson, which now became the center of the raging national controversy, the Freedom Riders sang a tune to the Calypso beat of "Banana Boat."

> We took a trip on the Greyhound Bus
> To fight segregation where we must
> Freedom, freedom, give us freedom!

Martin Luther King, Jr. watched the departure with mixed emotions. He was pleased, of course, by the evidence of government commitment. But it was not a good omen that so much effort, so much armor, was required to guarantee American citizens such a simple right. Although King's role in this venture was symbolic and tangential, he nevertheless played an important part in rallying public opinion. Not only white liberals but a large number of Negroes contended that Freedom Rider tactics were impractical and unduly provocative. As the leading American advocate of nonviolence and as a spokesman for the loosely-structured coordinating group, King ranged far and wide explaining and defending Freedom Rider groups. He denied charges that the Freedom Rides had materially damaged the Negro's cause. There was, of course, some undesirable reaction, but this was only the "creative tension" necessary for the birth of a new order. "I think all of this is unfortunate," King said, "but I think it is a psychological turning point in our whole struggle, just as Little Rock was a turning point in our legal struggle. The people themselves have said we can take it no longer. If we can get through this, I think it will mean breaking the backbone of massive resistance and discrimination."

But what of the oft-made charge that Freedom Riders were "outsiders?" King scoffed. "In a democracy and a nation that is tied together by many strains as a federal union, can we call anyone an outsider? It is as much my obligation as one who lives in Atlanta to be concerned by what takes place in Mississippi as it is that of a person who lives in Mississippi."

King was pleased but not diverted by an Interstate Commerce Commission order banning segregation in trains, buses, and supporting facilities. This order, though encouraging, did not meet head-on the basic issue of whether the federal government was ready, willing, and able to protect the rights of Negro citizens in Deep South areas. That issue, as King knew, had not been settled; it had only been postponed, pushed down to a deeper level of complexity. As chief spokesman and symbol of the cause, it fell to King to articulate this paradox and to rouse Negroes for a greater effort. As a student of history, he knew that human symbols were indispensable for focusing mass energy. "People cannot become devoted to Christianity," he said, "until they find Christ, to democracy until they find Lincoln and Jefferson and Roosevelt, to communism until they find Marx and Lenin and Stalin." What he was trying to explain here was the well-known historical fact "that people are often led to causes and often become committed to great ideas through persons who personify those ideas. They have to find the embodiment of the idea in flesh and blood in order to commit themselves to it."

Though King accepted the role thrust upon him, he told Mike Wallace on a WNTA-TV interview in February, 1961, that the role had distinct disadvantages. "When you are aware that you are a symbol, it causes you to search your soul constantly, to go through this job of self-analysis, to see if you live up to all of the high and noble principles that people surround you with, and to try at all times to keep the gulf between the public self and private self at a minimum—to bridge this gulf so that it serves at least to inspire the individual to rise from the is-ness of his present nature to the eternal ought-ness that forever confronts him. On the other hand, it has disadvantages in that you do lose some of your individual life, your private life. You lose some of the time that you would give to your family and to many of the other things that are important."

There was another disadvantage. To some people the word "symbol" suggested a man above the battle or at least a man on the edge of the battle. As the Negro rebellion spread, with other men bearing the brunt of action, criticism of King grew. The rising young students of the movement spoke openly and contemptuously of "the cult of personality." More concretely, they criticized King for failing to take a Freedom Ride into Mississippi. Patiently, wearily, King parried these thrusts. "I don't want to talk about my personal suffering," he said, "but I've been in jail as much as anyone in the movement. I think it would be a big mistake to try—as some civil rights leaders want to—to throw the students out of the movement. The little conflicts are inevitable. They arise as part of a shift of emphasis from the legal area to nonviolent direct action. These students are helping to deliver the rights that have been declared. We must overlook their impatience."

Although King turned away wrath with soft answers, he could not remain indifferent to the fact that his following was unravelling at the seams. Nor could he deny the charge that he was following, not leading; reacting, not acting—rushing from fire to fire blowing on other men's flames. As criticism mounted, King cast about for a defining act.

For some time now, he had been engaged in a tactical shift. Under the impact of the sit-ins and Freedom Rides, he had moved closer to pure Gandhism. The student rebels had borrowed the concept of confrontation from King and had carried it to a new level of development, adding mass to direct action. Now King lifted direct mass action from the students, articulating a new doctrine of citywide confrontations between Negro and white communities. Another factor of immense importance in the development of King's thinking was the growing effectiveness of the Southern Christian Leadership Conference. Since its founding in 1957, the conference had been hampered by frequent changes in personnel and policy. This period of programmatic and pragmatic confusion ended in 1960 with the employment of Wyatt Tee Walker as executive director. Lank, spare, a veteran of the sit-ins and the Freedom Rides, a Baptist minister like King, young, dapper, Walker proved to be adept not only in administration but also in tactical thinking and organizational in-fighting. It would be said later (by critics) that Walker tended to throw King's weight around, but it would also be said (by friends) that King, who found it difficult to say no, sorely needed someone at the time to do just that. Unlike Gandhi, who was passive with his enemies but demanded the right of absolute dictatorship over his aides and allies, King tended to withdraw from the chores no man can avoid if he wants the power to accomplish his purposes. With King's permission sometimes and sometimes without, Walker supplied the extra dimension, becoming to King what every great man needs—an indispensable aide who performs and takes the blame for organizationally vital chores. With Walker as a buffer and wedge, King and SCLC moved to the forefront of the struggle, attracting bright young rebels like James Bevel, Dorothy Cotton, and Andrew Young, who later became executive director. Additional organizational muscle was provided by Ralph D. Abernathy, now the pastor of an Atlanta church; James Lawson, the passionate advocate of pure Gandhism; and the Rev. Fred Shuttlesworth, the tough, wiry head of the SCLC affiliate in Alabama. By the fall of 1961, SCLC was honed to a fine fighting edge, lacking only an act and an opportunity to give it body and an identifiable posture.

King and the young men around him believed they saw the beginning of an opening in Albany, Georgia. In retrospect, it would appear that King and his aides overestimated the possibilities of the situation because of a felt need to act. However that may be, King's decision to enter Albany was an important step that laid the groundwork for a minor peak of the third phase of the developing Freedom movement.

The Albany movement grew out of a Freedom Ride into Albany in December, 1961, and the infiltration tactics of SNCC. The arrest of the Freedom Riders led to a local Albany movement which attracted King's attention. On the invitation of local leaders, King and his aides entered Albany in December and organized the Freedom movement's first mass confrontation.

The Albany demonstrations, like the Freedom Rides, introduced a new concept to the Freedom movement. What King wanted to do in Albany was to bring the full resources of the Negro community to bear in an across-the-board attack on the *system* of color-caste. What he demanded was not only integrated facilities but *the recognition of the Negro community* (i.e., the hiring of Negro policemen, the creation of a biracial committee, etc.).

How did he intend to *force* recognition?

By an encounter, by a frontal attack on the system, by a series of direct-action probes involving not tens or twenties but hundreds and, if possible, thousands.

The Negro community was prepared for this new departure in a series of mass meetings and nonviolent workshops. There then followed a series of mass marches on city halls, sit-ins at libraries and recreational outlets, and prayer vigils on downtown streets. King and some two thousand followers went to jail during the struggle which raged intermittently throughout the spring and summer of 1962. The arrest of King on three separate occasions and the arrest of several Northern clergymen and laymen created a mood of national concern but did not appreciably affect the outcome. Laurie Pritchett, the Albany chief of police, sapped the energy of the demonstrators by "legal defiance," i.e., the prompt and, to the television viewer, "peaceful" arrests of demonstrators for illegal assembly, unlawful parades, and disturbing the peace. Although this raised large questions about the use of local police power to frustrate constitutional provisions relating to peaceful assembly and federal court orders on segregated facilities, the federal government did not intervene.

Albany, by any standard, was a staggering defeat for King and the Freedom movement. The sit-ins and Freedom Rides had given men excessive confidence in the power of demonstrations, which are, in truth, useful instruments if used in the right place and within the right strategic framework. Many reasons have been cited by King and others for the Albany defeat, but few touch the essential problem. King allowed himself to be pushed into action, without adequate preparation, on a battlefield he did not choose with a faction-ridden army he never completely commanded.

For all that, the experience was not without value. Men learn to fight by fighting, by winning and losing—above all, by losing. King's career, before Albany, was an ascending staircase of successes. Now suddenly, he was a failure and men were saying in the great wide world beyond that nonviolence as a social issue was dead. Sobered, King withdrew to lick his wounds and think. At that point, in the darkest hour of his career, King proved what he had not yet proved: that he was a leader of authentic greatness.

In *The Hero in History*, Sidney Hook makes a sharp distinction between the leader who rises to fame as a result of events he did not create and the truly great leader who transcends events, men, and perhaps even time by creating not only his greatness but also the occasion of his greatness. No leader, of course, can create an event the time is not prepared for. But the genius of the great leader lies precisely in his apprehension of what the times require and in carrying through in the teeth of great opposition an act that changes the times. In Birmingham, King approached that kind of greatness, creating the occasion of the "Negro Revolution" by an act almost everyone said was ill-timed and ill-chosen.

Birmingham was to Albany what Greensboro was to Montgomery. Birmingham, in short, was a conscious act. It was *chosen*, not stumbled upon. It was created by a man who knew exactly what he wanted and how much he would probably have to pay to get it.

In the late summer of 1962, King decided to launch a series of Albany-type demonstrations in Birmingham. Profiting from the mistakes of Albany, King and his aides—principally Walker and Shuttlesworth —drew up a detailed battle plan and designated the forthcoming struggle "Project C." The "C" stood for confrontation, which was an accurate reflection of King's new vision of battle and of his understanding of the desires of voiceless Negroes driven to the edge of revolt by repeated disappointments and atrocities.

"Project C" was scheduled for the fall of 1962, but it was postponed by negotiations with the white power structure. By January, 1963, however, King was convinced that "creative tension" was necessary for racial progress in the South and in America. He felt, he said later, that "if Birmingham could be cracked, the direction of the entire nonviolent movement in the South could take a significant turn. It was our faith that 'as Birmingham goes, so goes the South.'" King's aide, the

Rev. Mr. Walker, added another reason, striking a silent chord in the hearts of millions of Negroes who were seeking a *relevant* celebration of the one-hundredth anniversary of the Emancipation Proclamation. "You've got to have a crisis to bargain with," he said. "To take a moderate approach hoping to get white help, doesn't work. They nail you to the cross, and it saps the enthusiasm of the followers. You've got to have a crisis."

Icily aware of the mistakes of the past and of the further fact that a defeat in Birmingham would probably wreck his career and the nonviolent crusade, King sent Walker and other SCLC aides to Birmingham to recruit workers secretly and to lay the groundwork for a crisis. Birmingham was involved just then in a mayoral election between Albert Boutwell, a "moderate" segregationist and T. Eugene (Bull) Connor, a rabid segregationist. It was decided therefore to postpone "Project C" until the election was decided. While waiting, King made a whirlwind tour, recruiting supporters and potential bail bond contributors in some sixteen cities. Though most of these activities transpired behind closed doors, King made a public declaration on January 31, 1963. A *Chicago Sun-Times* story of that date quoted him as saying he was preparing for "the most difficult campaign he [had] undertaken," an assault on racial segregation in Birmingham. He was now recruiting a "volunteer force," the story said, which would be notified several weeks before "B" day.

On "B" day, Wednesday, April 3, King opened the Birmingham campaign by announcing that he would lead demonstrations there until "Pharaoh lets God's people go." Specifically, King said, "Pharaoh" would have to establish fair hiring practices, a biracial committee, and desegregate facilities in downtown stores. In the "Birmingham Manifesto," King and his aides detailed the precipitating causes of the demonstrations.

> The patience of an oppressed people cannot endure forever. The Negro citizens of Birmingham for the last several years have hoped in vain for some evidence of good faith resolution of our just grievances.
>
> Birmingham is part of the United States and we are bona fide citizens. Yet the history of Birmingham reveals that very little of the democratic process touches the life of the Negro in Birmingham. We have been segregated racially, exploited economically, and dominated politi-

cally. Under the leadership of the Alabama Christian Movement for Human Rights, we sought relief by petition for the repeal of city ordinances requiring segregation and the institution of a merit hiring policy in city employment. We were rebuffed. We then turned to the system of the courts. We weathered set-back after set-back, with all of its costliness, finally winning the terminal, bus, parks and airport cases. The bus decision has been implemented begrudgingly and the parks decision prompted the closing of all municipally-owned recreational facilities with the exception of the zoo and Legion Field. The airport case has been a slightly better experience with the exception of hotel accommodations and the subtle discrimination that continues in the limousine service.

We have always been a peaceful people, bearing our oppression with super-human effort. Yet we have been the victims of repeated violence, not only that inflicted by the hoodlum element but also that inflicted by the blatant misuse of police power. Our memories are seared with painful mob experience of Mother's Day 1961 during the Freedom Ride. For years, while our homes and churches were being bombed, we heard nothing but the rantings and ravings of racist city officials.

The Negro protest for equality and justice has been a voice crying in the wilderness. Most of Birmingham has remained silent, probably out of fear. In the meanwhile, our city has acquired the dubious reputation of being the worst big city in race relations in the United States. Last fall, for a flickering moment, it appeared that sincere community leaders from religion, business and industry discerned the inevitable confrontation in race relations approaching. Their concern for the city's image and commonweal of all its citizens did not run deep enough. Solemn promises were made, pending a postponement of direct action, that we would be joined in a suit seeking the relief of segregation ordinances. Some merchants agreed to desegregate their rest-rooms as a good faith start, some actually complying, only to retreat shortly thereafter. We hold in our hands now, broken faith and broken promises.

We believe in the American Dream of democracy, in the Jeffersonian doctrine that "all men are created equal and are endowed by their Creator with certain inalienable rights, among these being life, liberty and the pursuit of happiness."

Twice since September we have deferred our direct action thrust in order that a change in city government would not be made in the hysteria of a community crisis. We act today in full concert with our

Hebraic-Christian tradition, the law of morality and the Constitution of our nation. The absence of justice and progress in Birmingham demands that we make a moral witness to give our community a chance to survive. We demonstrate our faith that we believe that the beloved community can come to Birmingham.

We appeal to the citizenry of Birmingham, Negro and white, to join us in this witness for decency, morality, self-respect and human dignity. Your individual and corporate support can hasten the day of "liberty and justice for all." This is Birmingham's moment of truth in which every citizen can play his part in her larger destiny. . . .

These were fine words if King could make them stick, but the odds were against him. The "Birmingham Manifesto" and the proposed demonstrations were denounced by many Negroes and most whites. Attorney General Kennedy said the move was ill-timed. Billy Graham questioned King's timing and called for a cooling-off period. Even worse, the Negro community of Birmingham was cool, if not hostile, feeling that King should have informed the local Negro power structure of the time and details of his proposed campaign.

King was taken aback by the sharpness of the criticism, but he pushed forward, sensing a new willingness in the Negro masses to walk a more dangerous road. The tactics of resistance embodied in "Project C," his plan for battle, rose in a calculated crescendo tied to the major events of the Easter season. King had learned in Albany and on other battlefields that a mass movement had to build to a climax and that a loss of momentum was usually fatal. For the first few days, therefore, he limited himself to probing operations (token sit-ins) designed primarily to feel out the opposition and to attract the attention of the Negro community. King's role in these opening salvos was minimal. He was preoccupied just then with his dangerously exposed flanks. From Wednesday, April 3, to Thursday, April 11, he traveled from meeting to meeting in a generally successful effort to soothe the ruffled feelings of the crucially important Negro leadership community. With his back against the wall, literally and figuratively, King explained the requirements of nonviolent warfare and the inadvisability of revealing to the enemy either the date or the details of a projected attack. Calling on every verbal resource at his command, King succeeded in convincing or at least silencing doubters and scoffers.

All the while, King and his aides held nightly mass meetings as morale boosters and channels of recruitment for the nonviolent army. Most important of all, as it turned out, James Bevel, a young Baptist minister in dungarees and a Jewish yarmelke, began to organize high school and grammar school students. To young and old, rich and poor, King and his aides emphasized the ten points of the "Commitment Blank".

COMMANDMENTS FOR THE VOLUNTEERS

I HEREBY PLEDGE MYSELF—MY PERSON AND BODY—TO THE NONVIOLENT MOVEMENT. THEREFORE I WILL KEEP THE FOLLOWING TEN COMMANDMENTS:

1. *Meditate* daily on the teachings and life of Jesus.
2. *Remember* always that the nonviolent movement in Birmingham seeks justice and reconciliation—not victory.
3. *Walk* and *Talk* in the manner of love for God is love.
4. *Pray* daily to be used by God in order that all men might be free.
5. *SACRIFICE* personal wishes in order that all men might be free.
6. *OBSERVE* with both friend and foe the ordinary rules of courtesy.
7. *SEEK* to perform regular service for others and for the world.
8. *REFRAIN* from the violence of fist, tongue or heart.
9. *STRIVE* to be in good spiritual and bodily health.
10. *FOLLOW* the directions of the movement and of the captain on a demonstration.

I sign this pledge, having seriously considered what I do and with the determination and will to persevere.

NAME ——————————————————
(Please print neatly)
ADDRESS ——————————————————
PHONE ——————————————————
NEAREST RELATIVE ——————————————
ADDRESS ——————————————————
Besides demonstrations, I could also help the Movement by:
(Circle the proper items)
Run errands, Drive my car, Fix food for volunteers, Clerical work, Make phone calls, Answer phones, Mimeograph, Type, Print signs; Distribute leaflets;

With his base secure, King raised the social ante, opening the second phase of the campaign with a token street demonstration. The next day, Palm Sunday, April 7, there was the first reconnaissance in force and the first open conflict between Negro demonstrators and white policemen who waded into the crowd with sticks and K-9 police dogs.

With the issue joined, King and his principal antagonist, Safety Commissioner "Bull" Connor, settled down to a war of attrition. King, aided by a strategy committee of twenty-four, operated from suite 30 in the Negro-owned and Negro-operated Gaston Motel. "Bull" Connor preferred the streets. Straw hat pulled down over one eye, in shirtsleeves, Connor operated from the barricades policemen and firemen posted near Negro churches to prevent demonstrators from reaching their strategic objective, city hall. After several skirmishes, both sides committed their major forces to the area surrounding the Kelly Ingram Park, a square block of elms, concrete, and ragged grass in the middle of the Negro business district. Across the street from this park was the yellow-brick structure of the Sixteenth Street Baptist Church which became the focal point of the struggle. As precautionary measures, "Bull" Connor ringed the area with wooden horses and applied to a local court for a restraining order. On Wednesday night, April 10, Judge W. A. Jenkins, Jr. issued a sweeping injunction barring almost every conceivable kind of protest, mass marches, boycotts and sit-ins. This injunction was served on King at 1:30 the next morning. King, moving closer to Gandhi, decided for the first time to openly defy a court order. Using Good Friday as a symbolic departure, he emerged from the Sixth Avenue Zion Hill Church at the head of a group of about forty demonstrators. King and his aide, Ralph Abernathy, were dressed in blue jeans and gray workshirts. Many of the marchers also wore old clothes to dramatize the Easter boycott King had called. Looking neither to the left nor right, his face grave and his manner solemn, King started marching toward the downtown section, followed by the small group of demonstrators and a crowd of one thousand onlookers who shouted: "Freedom has come to Birmingham!" As King and his group passed, some of the onlookers dropped to their knees. "Bull" Connor, his anger rising, allowed the demonstrators to march for seven or eight blocks before bellowing: "Stop 'em! Don't let them go any farther." King, Abernathy, and fifty-three demonstrators and onlookers were arrested.

King, by now, was used to jail. But the next few hours, he has said, "were the longest, most frustrating and bewildering . . . I have lived." He was separated almost immediately from Abernathy and placed in solitary confinement. "Having no contact of any kind," he wrote, "I was besieged with worry. How was the movement faring? Where would Fred [Shuttlesworth] and the others get the money to have our demonstrators released? What was happening to morale in the Negro community?"

Although King was not physically manhandled, he was intimidated somehow by his anxieties and the darkness of his cell. "In the mornings the sun would rise, sending shafts of light through the windows high in the narrow cell which was my home. You will never know the meaning of utter darkness until you have lain in such a dungeon, knowing that sunlight is streaming overhead and still seeing only darkness below. You might have thought I was in the grip of a fantasy brought on by worry. I did worry. But there was more to the blackness than a phenomenon conjured up by a worried mind. Whatever the case, the fact remained that I could not see the light."

Neither could Coretta King, who was convalescing from the birth of her fourth child, a girl, Bernice, on March 28. It was King's custom to call her immediately after an arrest. But two days had passed and there was no word from her husband, who, according to friends, was being held incommunicado. Not even his lawyers, it was said, had been able to see him. Was he alive? Had something happened to him? In mounting anxiety, she tried to reach President Kennedy at his Easter vacation headquarters in Palm Beach, Florida. The call was given to Press Secretary Pierre Salinger, who immediately called Robert F. Kennedy in Washington. The same day, Easter Sunday, April 14, Attorney General Kennedy called Coretta King and told her that he would contact Birmingham and "find out what the situation was." In a few hours, Robert Kennedy called back and said, according to Coretta, "that he wasn't successful in arranging a telephone call [but that her] husband was safe."

The next morning the local operator asked Coretta King, with some annoyance, to get her son Dexter, then two, off the telephone because the President of the United States was trying to reach her.

"When I had persuaded Dexter to desist," Coretta recalled, "I heard the familiar, sincere voice of the President. In his characteristically

On picket line in Atlanta,
passive resistance leader
talks with detective. King
was supporting student
campaign against chain
food store. Pickets said
store refused to hire Negro
clerks.

King is joined in protest
by the Rev. Samuel
Williams, then president
of the Atlanta NAACP.
Protest, one of many
King backed since
Montgomery boycott, oc-
curred in summer of 1960.

Handcuffed minister is led from Atlanta jail to DeKalb County court for hearing on traffic charge that played central role in 1960 Presidential campaign. DeKalb county judge sentenced King to four months in state prison.

swift manner, Mr. Kennedy asked: 'How are you, Mrs. King? I understand you talked with my brother yesterday. I'm sorry I couldn't call you personally, but, as you know, I was with our father. I wanted you to know that I have talked with Birmingham and arranged for your husband to call you. He'll be phoning shortly. Also, you might be interested in the fact that the FBI was sent in last night. They have talked with your husband. He's all right and we'll be keeping a check. They will remain there. I want you to feel free to call me or the Attorney General or Mr. Salinger if you have any concern at all. You know how to reach me, don't you?'

"Although all this was said," Coretta recalled, "in a rush of words, the President seemed in no hurry to get off the line. He was solicitous about my problems and my health. He said he was happy to learn that we had just had our fourth child. . . ."

The famous Kennedy touch solved King's personal problems but did not alter significantly the correlation of forces involved in the Birmingham struggle. Alone in jail, King began to think deeply about the forces arrayed against him. He was particularly concerned about a widely-publicized letter circulated by eight leading white ministers of Birmingham—Roman Catholic, Jewish, Protestant—who denounced King as an interloper and extremist. The churchmen had urged "our own Negro community to withdraw support" from these "unwise and untimely" demonstrations. With time on his hands, King considered this and other critical evaluations of his work. As he thought, other questions came to his mind. What was he trying to do? Was it morally justifiable? Who was he? King sat down in his cell and composed a nine-thousand-word letter which became a classic of the civil rights movement. Let us consider the "Letter from a Birmingham Jail" in some detail for it is by far the most incisive and eloquent statement of his racial philosophy. King considered first the doctrine of the "outsider." Why was he, an Atlantan, in Birmingham?

> . . . I am here, along with several members of my staff, because we were invited here. I am here because I have basic organizational ties here.
> Beyond this, I am in Birmingham because injustice is here. Just as the eighth century prophets left their little villages and carried their "thus saith the Lord" far beyond the boundaries of their hometowns;

and just as the Apostle Paul left his little village of Tarsus and carried the gospel of Jesus Christ to practically every hamlet and city of the Graeco-Roman world, I, too, am compelled to carry the gospel of freedom beyond my particular hometown. Like Paul, I must constantly respond to the Macedonian call for aid.

Turning now to the recurring criticism of his timing, King told the white churchmen of Alabama:

> . . . My friends, I must say to you that we have not made a single gain in civil rights without determined legal and nonviolent pressure. History is the long and tragic story of the fact that privileged groups seldom give up their unjust posture; but as Reinhold Niebuhr has reminded us, groups are more immoral than individuals.
>
> We know through painful experience that freedom is never voluntarily given by the oppressor; it must be demanded by the oppressed. Frankly, I have never yet engaged in a direct action movement that was "well-timed" according to the timetable of those who have not suffered unduly from the disease of segregation. For years now I have heard the word "Wait." It rings in the ear of every Negro with a piercing familiarity. This "Wait" has always meant "Never." It has been a tranquilizing thalidomide, relieving the emotional stress for a moment only to give birth to an ill-formed infant of frustration. We must come to see with the distinguished jurist of yesterday that "justice too long delayed is justice denied." We have waited for more than three hundred and forty years for our constitutional and God-given rights.

But why direct action?
Why not litigation?
Why not negotiation?

> . . . You are exactly right in your call for negotiation. Indeed, this is the purpose of direct action. Nonviolent direct action seeks to create such a crisis and establish such creative tension that a community that has consistently refused to negotiate is forced to confront the issue. It seeks so to dramatize the issue that it can no longer be ignored. I just referred to the creation of tension as a part of the work of the nonviolent register. This may sound rather shocking. But I must confess that I am not afraid of the word tension. I have earnestly worked and

Under direction of King and other leaders, Freedom Riders hold nonviolent workshop in home of Montgomery druggist. Riders held three-day training session before leaving for Jackson, Mississippi.

Negro Freedom Riders, including the Rev. A. D. King (l.), Martin Luther King's brother, eat breakfast at lunch counter in Montgomery bus station before leaving for Jackson, Mississippi.

Seeking spiritual guidance before continuing trip, Freedom Riders bow heads in prayer. SCLC, SNCC, CORE, and other organizations were involved in second stage of Freedom Rides which created national controversy.

As chairman and spokesman of the Freedom Ride Coordinating Committee, King bids goodbye to Freedom Rider Paul Dietrich at the Montgomery bus station.

Freedom Ride continued on May 24 with group including James Farmer (with briefcase). First bus of Freedom Riders was accompanied by two battalions of national guardsmen, highway patrolmen, three reconnaisance planes, and helicopter.

James Zwerg, a white student from Nashville, removes shattered teeth from mouth after brutal beating at Montgomery bus station on May 20, 1961. John Lewis (l.), another Freedom Rider, later became national chairman of SNCC.

preached against violent tension, but there is a type of constructive nonviolent tension that is necessary for growth. Just as Socrates felt that it was necessary to create a tension in the mind so that individuals could rise from the bondage of myths and half-truths to the unfettered realm of creative analysis and objective appraisal, we must see the need of having nonviolent gadflies to create the kind of tension in society that will help men to rise from the dark depths of prejudice and racism to the majestic heights of understanding and brotherhood. So the purpose of direct action is to create a situation so crisis-packed that it will inevitably open the door to negotiation. . . .

King turned now to the most vulnerable point in his nonviolent posture. Gandhi had urged his followers to disobey *all* laws of the British colonial government. His philosophical position grew out of a declaration that the government itself was null and void.

King, on the other hand, had been forced by the exigencies of the American situation to urge men to obey some laws and to disobey others. How justify this?

. . . The answer is found in the fact that there are two types of laws: There are *just* laws and there are *unjust* laws. I would agree with Saint Augustine that "An unjust law is no law at all."

Now what is the difference between the two? How does one determine when a law is just or unjust? A just law is a man-made code that squares with the moral law or the law of God. An unjust law is a code that is out of harmony with the moral law. To put it in the terms of Saint Thomas Aquinas, an unjust law is a human law that is not rooted in eternal and natural law. Any law that uplifts human personality is just. Any law that degrades human personality is unjust. All segregation statutes are unjust because segregation distorts the soul and damages the personality. . . .

Let us turn to a more concrete example of just and unjust laws. An unjust law is a code that a majority inflicts on a minority that is not binding on itself. This is *difference* made legal. On the other hand, a just law is a code that a majority compels a minority to follow that it is willing to follow itself. This is *sameness* made legal.

Let me give another explanation. An unjust law is a code inflicted upon a minority which that minority had no part in enacting or creating because they did not have the unhampered right to vote. Who can say that the legislature of Alabama which set up the segregation laws was democratically elected? Throughout the state of Alabama all types of devious methods are used to prevent Negroes from becoming registered voters and there are some counties without a single Negro registered to vote despite the fact that the Negroes constitute a majority of the population. Can any law set up in such a state be considered democratically structured?

These are just a few examples of unjust and just laws. There are some instances when a law is just on its face and unjust in its application. For instance, I was arrested Friday on a charge of parading without a permit. Now there is nothing wrong with an ordinance which requires a permit for a parade, but when the ordinance is used to preserve segregation and to deny citizens the First Amendment privilege of peaceful assembly and peaceful protest, then it becomes unjust.

I hope you can see the distinction I am trying to point out. In no sense do I advocate evading or defying the law as the rabid segregationist would do This would lead to anarchy. One who breaks an unjust law must do it openly, lovingly. . . . I submit that an individual who breaks a law that conscience tells him is unjust, and willingly accepts the penalty by staying in jail to arouse the conscience of the community over its injustice, is in reality expressing the very highest respect for law. . . .

. . . We can never forget that everything Hitler did in Germany was "legal" and everything the Hungarian freedom fighters did in Hungary was "illegal."

King went on to confess his great disappointment with white moderates, white liberals, and white Christians ("Who is their God?"). Then, coming closer to the matter at hand, he defined himself as a "creative extremist" who stood, paradoxically, "in the middle."

You spoke of our activity in Birmingham as extreme. At first I was rather disappointed that fellow clergymen would see my nonviolent

As political leader, King helped organize "Freedom March" on Democratic National Convention in Los Angeles. King and Roy Wilkins led some five thousand marchers who walked to Shrine Auditorium where they listened to Presidential candidates give their views on civil rights.

Addressing crowd, King calls for forthright responses from the Presidential candidates. In background are Wilkins and Paul Butler, then Democratic national chairman.

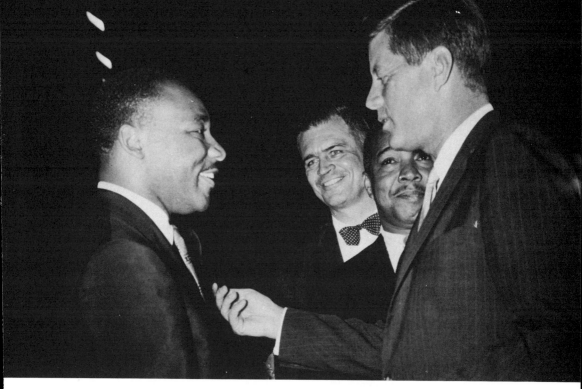

Senator John F. Kennedy, who later won nomination, exchanges quips with King at Shrine Auditorium. King later played a central role in the election of Senator Kennedy. Most students believe Kennedy's call to King's wife to express sympathy over arrest of her husband swayed enough votes to win the bitterly-contested 1960 campaign.

efforts as those of the extremist. I started thinking about the fact that I stand in the middle of two opposing forces in the Negro community. One is a force of complacency made up of Negroes who, as a result of long years of oppression, have been so completely drained of self-respect and a sense of "somebodiness" that they have adjusted to segregation, and, on the other hand, of a few Negroes in the middle class who, because of a degree of academic and economic security and because at points they profit by segregation, have unconsciously become insensitive to the problems of the masses. The other force is one of bitterness, and hatred and comes perilously close to advocating violence. It is expressed in the various black nationalist groups that are springing up over the nation, the largest and best known being Elijah Muhammad's Muslim movement. This movement is nourished by the contemporary frustration over the continued existence of racial discrimination. It is made up of people who have lost faith in America, who have absolutely repudiated Christianity, and who have concluded that the white man is an incurable "devil." I have tried to stand between these two forces saying that we need not follow the "do-nothingism" of the complacent or the hatred and despair of the black nationalist. There is a more excellent way of love and nonviolent protest. I'm grateful to God that, through the Negro church, the dimension of nonviolence entered our struggle. If this philosophy had not emerged I am convinced that by now many streets of the South would be flowing with blood. And I am further convinced that if our white brothers dismiss as "rabble rousers" and "outside agitators" those of us who are working through the channels of nonviolent direct action, and refuse to support our nonviolent efforts, millions of Negroes, out of frustration and despair, will seek solace and security in black nationalist ideologies, a development that will lead inevitably to a frightening racial nightmare. . . .

But, as I continued to think about the matter, I gradually gained a bit of satisfaction from being considered an extremist. Was not Jesus an extremist in love—"Love your enemies, bless them that curse you, pray for them that despitefully use you." Was not Amos an extremist for justice—"Let justice roll down like waters and righteousness like a mighty stream." Was not Paul an extremist for the gospel of Jesus Christ—"I bear in my body the marks of the Lord Jesus." Was not Abraham Lincoln an extremist—"This nation cannot survive half slave and half free." Was not Thomas Jefferson an extremist—"We hold these truths to be self evident that all men are created equal." So the question is not whether we will be extremist, but what kind of extremist will we be? Will we be extremists for hate or will we be extremists for love? Will we be extremists for the preservation of injustice, or will we be extremists for the cause of justice? In that dramatic scene on Calvary's hill, three men were crucified. We must never forget that all three were crucified for the same crime of extremism. Two were extremists for immorality, and thusly fell below their environment. The other Jesus Christ was an extremist for love, truth, and goodness, and thereby rose above his environment. So, after all, maybe the South, the nation and the world are in dire need of creative extremists.

There shone in these words qualities more manifest than sincerity. What King was saying, philosophical considerations apart, was that he was committed to a fight to the finish and that sooner or later somebody was going to have to do something about it. King emphasized that fact four days later by posting bond and resuming direction of the flagging movement. For a brief spell, King faced the very real possibility of another Albany. But the King of Birmingham was not the King of Albany. His moves now were informed by a deeper strategic insight. The terrain of Birmingham, moreover, was more favorable to his purposes. Birmingham, unlike Albany, was a key industrial center, and men could not long remain indifferent to what happened there. Another element in the Birmingham equation was "Bull" Connor, who blundered into King's hands by using tactics (fire hoses and police dogs) that went beyond the "polite repression" America had become accustomed to. John F. Kennedy said later that "the civil rights movement owes "Bull" Connor as much as it owes Abraham Lincoln."

The movement owes even more to Negro children. As the month of May approached, it became clear to King that a truly decisive act was necessary to counter the dangerous seepage of enthusiasm. More and more, as the days wore away with inconclusive adult demonstrations, one question hammered insistently on King's mind: "What are you going to do about the children?" The question had obtruded itself early. James Bevel and other SCLC aides had recruited an enthusiastic cadre of students, who were demanding assignment to the front lines. King had used children in Albany under different circumstances. But the question before him now was the advisability of committing children en masse to a potentially explosive struggle. The question was hammered out in a series of meetings in suite 30. It is easy, in retrospect, as I have written elsewhere, to say that the decision they made was brilliant. But the sun was hooded by clouds then and few men were willing to assume the awesome responsibility for the possible death of a child. Many men said later that they made the big decision. But back there, it was all in one man's hands, and history will note that sometime before May 2, 1963, Martin Luther King, Jr., gave his assent to one of the most momentous decisions in the history of Negro protests. In that hour, eyes red from lack of sleep, he took upon his shoulders the awful burden of committing thousands of children to the front lines of a battle that was being fought (by policemen and firemen) with billy clubs, fierce dogs, and water hoses that could strip bark from an oak tree.

Thursday, May 2, dawned, hot and muggy. "Bull" Connor was waiting, shortly after 1:00 P.M., when some one thousand Negro youths poured out of the Sixteenth Street Baptist Church and advanced, singing and shouting, on the barricades of Birmingham. This was more than a demonstration; it was an explosion. The young Negro demonstrators in squads of ten and fifty fanned out in several directions, penetrating police lines and reaching the downtown section. In all, some one thousand youths were arrested. The next day, Friday, an even larger crowd flocked to the field of battle, leaving Negro schools virtually empty. Savagely now, King increased the pressure, sending wave after wave into the maw of the battle. In desperation, "Bull" Connor counterattacked, bowling the children, some no older than six or seven, over with high-powered hoses. Policemen then waded in with sticks and dogs, enraging adult onlookers, who responded with a barrage of bricks and bottles.

With a rush now, sentiment changed. Pictures of police dogs biting Negro children circled the globe, revolting millions. Senator Wayne Morse (D., Oregon) told the U.S. Senate that the repression of Birmingham "would disgrace a Union of South Africa or a Portuguese Angola." The New York Times said editorially that the Birmingham "barbarities" were "revoltingly reminiscent of totalitarian excesses." Of greater consequence was the impact of all this on black Birmingham, which became a solid mass of defiance and discontent. King had his crisis and he escalated it, day by day, announcing that he had no intention of relaxing the pressure. "We are ready to negotiate," he said. "But we intend to negotiate from strength. If the white power structure of this city will meet some of our minimum demands, then we will consider calling off the demonstrations, but we want promises, plus action."

On Monday and Tuesday, May 6-7, the demonstrations reached unprecedented intensity and Birmingham teetered on the edge of total social disorder. By that time, Birmingham jails were filled with some two thousand demonstrators and law enforcement facilities were strained to the breaking point. After the Tuesday demonstration, Sheriff Melvin Bailey of Jefferson County told a group of seventy leading business and civic leaders that it would be necessary to impose martial law if the demonstrations were not ended. The white community leaders immediately empowered a committee to come to terms with Negro leaders. On Friday, May 10, after a marathon negotiating session, King and his top Birmingham aide, Fred Shuttlesworth, announced agreement on a phased program which called for desegregation of lunch counters, restrooms, fitting rooms and drinking fountains, fair hiring practices, and the release of demonstrators on nominal bonds. "The City of Birmingham," King and Shuttlesworth announced, somewhat prematurely, "has come to an accord with its conscience."

Enraged segregationists struck back immediately, bombing Gaston Motel and the home of King's brother, the Rev. A. D. King, on Saturday night, May 11. The remaining hours of darkness posed a severe test for King and nonviolence. Thousands of Negro adults poured into the streets, stoning policemen and firemen. During the riot, which lasted until the early hours of the morning, scores of cars were destroyed, torches were put to stores and two apartment houses, a policeman and a cab driver were stabbed, and some fifty others were injured. King, who was resting in Atlanta, dashed to the city and made what was called a "poolroom pilgrimage" in an attempt to pacify the populace. President Kennedy alerted U.S. armed forces, but the disturbance died down without further incident. Though the Birmingham riot was not a repudiation of King's nonviolent philosophy, it indicated clearly that he faced serious problems, particularly in the so-called underclass, the permanently-depressed strata at the bottom of the Negro working

Demonstrators hold "prayer vigil" on sidewalks of
Albany, Georgia, where King led antisegregation
campaign from December, 1961, to August, 1962. As in
other cities, he called for desegregation of public
facilities, establishment of a biracial committee, and
hiring of Negro policemen.

In Albany jail, King greets reporters after using telephone in police chief's office to cancel speaking engagements. He was arrested on July 27, 1962, in a "prayer vigil" in front of city hall.

After release from jail on August 10, King discusses situation with wife Coretta. He was jailed three times in Albany.

class. The only consolation King could derive from the riot was that the rioters were not active members of the Birmingham crusade and that the riot itself would probably have been a great deal worse had he not made nonviolence central to the posture of Birmingham demonstrators.

Standing now at the peak of his career, King made a triumphant tour, speaking to 25,000 in Los Angeles, 10,000 in Chicago, leading some 125,000 in a phenomenal Detroit "Freedom Walk." Even as King made his way across the country, the fire he had lighted in Birmingham leaped from ghetto to ghetto, igniting charges of social energy and welding Negroes of all ranks and creeds into a mass of indignation. With a despair born of one hundred years of oppression, with new hope born of Birmingham, Negroes exploded in the streets of America, sprawling in front of cars and bulldozers, standing-in, sitting-in, marching, singing, shouting: "Freedom Now!"

Men in the mass are taught not by books but by events. As Nehru said: "A mass struggle . . . is the best and swiftest method, though perhaps a painful one, of giving political education to the masses. For the masses need the 'schooling of big events.' Ordinary peace-time political activity, such as elections in democratic countries, often confuses the average person. There is a deluge of oratory, and every candidate promises all manner of fine things, and the poor voter, or the man in the field or factory or shop, is confused. There are no very clear lines of cleavage for him between one group and another. But when a mass struggle comes, or in time of revolution, the real position stands out clearly, as if lit up by lightning. In such moments of crisis, groups or classes or individuals cannot hide their real feelings or character. Truth will out. Not only is a time of revolution a test of character, of courage, endurance, and selflessness, it also brings out the real conflicts between different classes and groups, which had so far been covered up by fine and vague phrases."

Schooled by "big events," by Montgomery, Greensboro, Albany and, above all, Birmingham, the Negro people of America rose up in 1963 in a revolt of unprecedented intensity. As the fires of crisis glowed and flickered across the land, Martin Luther King reached a point of eminence no other Negro has known. A *Newsweek* magazine survey, published July 29, 1963, noted that King received an 88 per cent favorable rating from the Negro masses and a 95 per cent favorable response from the one hundred leaders in the sample. To be sure, there were friendly critics like SNCC leader Horace Julian Bond, who said that King had "sold the concept that one man will come to your town and save you," and James Baldwin, who said that King had great appeal but "no moral authority" in the concrete ghettos of the North. There was also continuing criticism of King's emphasis on love; but, by and large, most Negro and white Americans regarded King as the symbol and chief spokesman for what was by now called the "Negro Revolution."

King made no immediate effort to translate his appeal into the national movement, but he did express great satisfaction with the mounting militancy of urban Negroes. He was pleased also by the new level of white commitment that followed the epochal Birmingham struggle. Even more encouraging was the emergence of what King called "a new" John F. Kennedy. Recognizing the call of history, Kennedy made an abrupt turn and accepted the mantle of moral leadership King had urged upon him. Not only did Kennedy organize the energies of business, labor, and church leadership, he also became the first American President to take the official position that segregation was morally wrong. Speaking on June 11, 1963, on the eve of the assassination of Medgar Evers, the Mississippi NAACP leader, Kennedy said: "One hundred years of delay have passed since President Lincoln freed the slaves, yet their heirs, their grandsons are not fully free. They are not yet freed from the bonds of injustice; they are not yet freed from social and economic oppression. And this nation, for all its hopes and its boasts will not be fully free until all its citizens are free." The President concluded:

> We preach freedom around the world, and we mean it. And we cherish our freedom here at home. But are we to say to the world—and much more importantly to each other—that this is the land of the free, except for the Negroes; that we have no second-class citizens, except for Negroes; that we have no class or caste system, no ghettos, no master race, except with respect to Negroes?
>
> Now the time has come for this nation to fulfill its promise. The events in Birmingham and elsewhere have so increased the cries for equality that no city or state or legislative body can prudently choose to ignore them.

The fires of frustration and discord are burning in every city, North and South. . . . We face, therefore, a moral crisis as a country and a people. It cannot be met by repressive police action. It cannot be left to increased demonstrations in the streets. It cannot be quieted by token moves or talk. It is a time to act in the Congress, in your state and local legislative body, and, above all, in all of our daily lives. . . .

Those who do nothing are inviting shame as well as violence. Those who act boldly are recognizing right as well as reality. . . .

Listening to these words, which he called "the most earnest, human and profound appeal for understanding and justice that any President has uttered since the first days of the Republic," King perceived the *beginning* of a government breakthrough as significant in its own way as the Birmingham breakthrough which prepared the way for it. Kennedy's next act, the submission to the Congress of the most far-ranging civil rights bill since Reconstruction, confirmed King's hopes. Equally encouraging was the new ferment in the white Christian church.

All these currents mingled in the March on Washington which brought 250,000 persons, some 60,000 of them white, to Lincoln's Monument in history's largest civil rights demonstration. The March was, in essence, a return on a higher level of effectiveness to the Prayer Pilgrimage of 1957 and, like the Prayer Pilgrimage, it marked a milestone in King's development as a national Negro leader. The March was sponsored by a broad spectrum of groups and King shared leadership with Wilkins, Randolph, James Farmer of CORE, John Lewis of SNCC, Whitney Young of the Urban League, Walter Reuther of the UAW-CIO, and Eugene Carson Blake of the Presbyterian Church. It was King, however, that the crowd came to see; and it was King who brought the throng to its feet with the most eloquent address of his career. King came on last, after a long day of songs and speeches, and he read for a time from a prepared speech. One hundred years had passed, he said, and the Negro was still not free. "*One hundred years later,* the life of the Negro is still sadly crippled by the manacles of segregation, and the chains of discrimination. *One hundred years later,* the Negro lives on a lonely island of poverty in the midst of a vast ocean of material prosperity. *One hundred years later,* the Negro is still languishing in the corners of American society and finds himself an exile in his own land. *One hundred years later.* . . ."

The demonstrators, King said, looking out over a crowd that covered both sides of the reflecting pool and stretched almost a mile to the east, were there to "cash a check." The Founding Fathers in the Declaration of Independence and the Constitution had signed a promissory note to which every American was to fall heir. But America had defaulted on her obligation. "Instead of honoring this sacred obligation, America has given the Negro people a bad check; a check which has come back marked 'insufficient funds.'" The crowd, warming to King, applauded this verbal thrust, and King hurried on, saying there would be no rest, no peace, no "cooling off" until the obligation was honored. "1963," he said, "is not an end, but a beginning. Those who hope that the Negro needed to blow off steam and will now be content will have a rude awakening if the nation returns to business as usual." King warned against hate and bitterness. "We cannot," he said, "walk alone." Yet, with "our white brothers," when possible, and without them if necessary, "we shall march ahead. We cannot turn back. . . . We can never be satisfied as long as a Negro in Mississippi cannot vote and a Negro in New York believes he has nothing for which to vote." Still reading, King praised "the veterans of creative suffering" and urged them to continue to work with the faith that unearned suffering is redemptive.

"Go back to Mississippi, go back to Alabama, go back to Georgia, go back to Louisiana, go back to the slums and ghettos of our Northern cities, knowing that somehow this situation can and will be changed. . . ."

King turned his eyes now from the paper on the lectern to the crowd before him, from the strife of the battle to the victory ahead. Digging deep within himself, picking up bits and fluffs of speeches dating back to 1956, he began to improvise, rolling out long, legato phrases that brought cheers like thunderous waves from the massive crowd. Despite everything, despite "the difficulties and frustrations of the moment," "he had a dream," he said, of a day when the rough places would be made plain and the sons of former slaveowners and the sons of former slaves would sit down together at the table of brotherhood. Over and over again, King repeated the rhythmical phrase, "I have a dream today," and the throng, electrified, rose en masse, screaming, cheering, and crying, pushing him to ascending heights of revelation and discovery.

Medgar Evers, NAACP field secretary for Mississippi, is pictured in Jackson office before his assassination by white segregationist. King said the shooting was "a political assassination." The murder of Evers was one of several violent incidents that marred the centennial celebration of the Emancipation Proclamation.

King (l.) and Roy Wilkins of NAACP (c.) led distinguished group of mourners who assembled in
Jackson for Evers' rites. Near-riot was narrowly averted
after leaders and other mourners staged a solemn mass
march through downtown Jackson.

I have a dream that my four little children will one day live in a nation where they will not be judged by the color of their skin but by the content of their character.

I have a dream today.

I have a dream that one day the state of Alabama, whose governor's lips are presently dripping with the words of interposition and nullification, will be transformed into a situation where little black boys and black girls will be able to join hands with little white boys and white girls and walk together as sisters and brothers.

I have a dream today.

I have a dream that one day every valley shall be exalted, every hill and mountain shall be made low, the rough places will be made plain, and the crooked places will be made straight, and the glory of the Lord shall be revealed, and all flesh shall see it together.

This is our hope. This is the faith with which I return to the South. With this faith we will be able to hew out of the mountain of despair a stone of hope. With this faith we will be able to transform the jangling discords of our nation into a beautiful symphony of brotherhood. With this faith we will be able to work together, to pray together, to struggle together, to go to jail together, to stand up for freedom together, knowing that we will be free one day.

This will be the day when all of God's children will be able to sing with new meaning "My country 'tis of thee, sweet land of liberty, of thee I sing. Land where my fathers died, land of the pilgrim's pride, from every mountainside, let freedom ring."

And if America is to be a great nation this must become true. So let freedom ring from the prodigious hilltops of New Hampshire! Let freedom ring from the mighty mountains of New York! Let freedom ring from the heightening Alleghenies of Pennsylvania!

Let freedom ring from the snowcapped Rockies of Colorado!

Let freedom ring from the curvaceous peaks of California!

But not only that; let freedom ring from Stone Mountain of Georgia!

Let freedom ring from every hill and mole hill of Mississippi. From every mountainside, let freedom ring.

When we let freedom ring, when we let it ring from every village and every hamlet, from every state and every city, we will be able to speed up that day when all of God's children, black men and white men, Jews and Gentiles, Protestants and Catholics, will be able to join hands and sing in the words of that old Negro spiritual, "Free at last! Free at last! Thank God almighty, we are free at last!"

When King finished, grown men and women stood in the shadow of the leaves and wept uncontrollably. King's speech had an impact on its age not unlike the totally different speech of Booker T. Washington sixty-eight years before. Major Northern papers and periodicals quoted it extensively and many added editorially that it was "a masterpiece." Even more important, King's words were carried via electronic devices to millions more in America, Africa, Asia, and Europe.

Splendid as the words were, they nevertheless fell short of King's own high standards. For standing there in the hollow of a million hearts, with all the world watching and listening, he focused primarily on ends and not means, lifting's men's eyes from the shot and grape of battle to the heavens beyond, where there was milk and cool water and honey. This approach, though of immense value from the standpoint of internal morale and external public relations, left King open to the criticism of events.

The bells of freedom did not ring. Eighteen days later Martin Luther King, Jr., and millions of other Americans were mortified by a revolting atrocity. A car sped down Sixteenth Street and a hand tossed a bomb into the Sixteenth Street Baptist Church, which was filled with Sunday school students, some of whom never knew what hit them. Four girls died in the blast and twenty-one were injured. Later that day, two other Negroes were killed, one by a policeman. King again dashed to the city which again trembled on the edge of social disaster. It was doubtless through King's influence and the influence of the Rev. Mr. Shuttlesworth and other nonviolent leaders that a violent explosion was averted. But the patience of the Negroes of Birmingham and of America was sorely tried by this episode, and King, standing in the eye of the hurricane, was uneasily aware of that fact and of America's apparent unawareness of it. Gene Grove, of the *New York Post*, saw him standing, outwardly calm, in the Sixth Avenue Baptist Church on the occasion of the funeral of the four victims. ". . . Martin Luther King," he wrote, "looked down over the mountain of flowers at a ray of sunshine which pierced a window on his left and laid his hand upon Cynthia's [Wesley] casket. Dr. King said the girls were 'martyrs of a holy crusade for human dignity. They have something to say to all of us, to ministers safe behind stained glass windows, to politicians who feed their constituents the stale bread of hatred and the spoiled meat of racism. . . .' "

The traumatic shock of the Birmingham bombing changed the texture of the Negro mood and intensified the pressures on King. On all sides now, men raised demands for open civil disobedience. Radical student activists called for the recruitment of a civil rights army of twenty-five thousand and the launching of a total civil disobedience campaign (nonpayment of state and local taxes, strikes, and the blockading of transportation facilities) in Alabama. The plan, as revealed by Lawrence Still of *Jet* and Wallace Terry of the *Washington Post*, called for demonstrators to declare that "within our conscience" the white state government was "null and void." There was a similar ferment in the North, where James Baldwin called for open civil disobedience. Baldwin and a group of New York writers and artists (John O. Killens, Ruby Dee, Ossie Davis, Louis E. Lomax, and others) later urged a total Christmas boycott.

King, who is both practical and idealistic, was not at all sure that the moment had come for a full-scale civil disobedience campaign. But, significantly, he permitted his chief assistant, Wyatt Tee Walker, to send up a trial balloon. "The question is," Walker said, "whether we want to continue local guerilla battles against discimination and segregation or go to all-out war." Walker went on to ask in a speech to the SCLC convention: ". . . has the moment come in the development of the nonviolent revolution that we are forced [by delays and painfully slow results] . . . on some appointed day or some appointed hour [to] literally immobilize the nation until she acts on our pleas for justice and morality that have been too long denied. Is the day far-off that major transportation centers would be deluged with mass acts of civil disobedience; airports, train stations, bus terminals, the traffic of large cities, interstate commerce, would be halted by the bodies of witnesses nonviolently insisting on 'Freedom Now.' I suppose a nationwide work stoppage might attract enough attention to persuade someone to do something to get this monkey of segregation and discrimination off our backs, once, now and forever. Will it take one or all of these?"

King was persuaded finally by the pressure of events and the conflicting priorities of his allies that the time was not ripe for any of these departures. He has been criticized, perhaps too harshly, for not *leading* the rebellion he had created. It has been said that the movement of 1963 faltered because it lacked a dynamizing center, because too many men in too many places were creating acts that were not joined to each other or to a coherent national pattern or purpose. While this is true, it is certainly true also that it would have been difficult, if not impossible, for any one man to force the separate streams of the rebellion into one broad current. In *Why We Can't Wait*, King entered a general demurrer to the charges of his critics. "My preference," he wrote, "would have been to resume demonstrations in the wake of the September bombing, and I strongly urged militant action without delay. But some of those in our movement held other views. Against the formidable adversaries we faced, the fullest unity was indispensable, and I yielded." It seems also that King was hampered by his membership in the national Negro summit group, a coordinating structure of militants, moderates, and activists (NAACP, National Urban League, CORE, SNCC, SCLC) whose voices and conflicting priorities checkmated each other. King strongly endorsed the proposed Christmas boycott, but backed down publicly in the face of determined opposition from the militantly-moderate members of the national directorate.

Whatever the cause, King rested on the richly deserved laurels of Birmingham. In the remaining months of 1963, his attention was diffused over two complementary facets of the same reality, the rising wrath of Negroes and the rising fear of whites. As the resistance movement rose in the North, attitudes hardened on both sides of the racial lines and within contending groups in the Negro and white communities. The generalized Northern attacks on *de facto* school and housing segregation were followed by a "white backlash," a euphemism for the surfacing and open articulation of latent bigotry. The surfacing of anti-Negro hysteria was clearly apparent in low-income white groups, but it was not confined to these segments, as the precipitous drop in President Kennedy's popularity indicated.

This development, though menacing, did not surprise King. He told reporters that "demonstrations in such cities as New York and Chicago aroused the ire of many persons in the North. But the Negro revolution has revealed to many persons in the North that they had more deep-seated prejudices than they realized." What was even more revealing, King thought, was the extent to which hatred of the Negro had affected the moral fiber of the nation. He had warned many times before that hate was "a contagion," that it irradiated throughout a society, contaminating and affecting everything it touched.

In King's view, the assassination of President Kennedy was a direct result of this "morally inclement climate." Like all American Negroes and almost all whites, he was horrified by the deed, which contradicted the spirit and meaning of his own life. To King, as to other Negroes, the emerging Kennedy had become a locus of hope. And now, suddenly, inexplicably, he was dead—shot down in the prime of life by an assassin. Unbidden, King's mind went back to his own brush with death and forward to the ever-present possibility of an attempt on his own life. To reporters, King articulated a theory of national responsibility which he later reduced to writing. "While the question 'who killed President Kennedy?' is important, the question 'what killed him?' is more important. Our late President was assassinated by a morally inclement climate. It is a climate filled with heavy torrents of false accusation, jostling winds of hatred and raging storms of violence.

"It is a climate where men cannot disagree without being disagreeable, and where they express dissent through violence and murder. It is the same climate that murdered Medgar Evers in Mississippi and six innocent Negro children in Birmingham, Alabama. So in a sense we are all participants in that horrible act that tarnished the image of our nation. By our silence, by our willingness to compromise principle; by our constant attempt to cure the cancer of racial injustice with the vaseline of graduation; our readiness to allow arms to be purchased at will and fired at whim; by allowing our movie and television screens to teach our children that the hero is one who masters the art of shooting and the technique of killing; by allowing all of these developments we have created an atmosphere in which violence and hatred have become popular pastimes."

As a symbol of love, hope, and the denial of charity, King was one of 1,200 invited guests who crammed into Washington's St. Matthew's Cathedral for the Kennedy funeral. During the Mass, he sat somber and thoughtful, marveling not for the first time that week on the whirligigs of fate. He had come, over the years, to know Kennedy and to admire and respect him as a friend. They had a great deal in common, the two men, both young, both eloquent, both ambitious. Had not one been in jail the other might not have been President and might not now be dead. Such was fate of which King had spoken that year over other caskets, in other places. Sitting here now in the shadow of a deed of violence, King was reminded afresh of the realness of evil which contrasted so sharply with his image of Kennedy whose lengthening shadow told him that good also was real and even in death would abide. It seemed to King that the dead President spoke to all Americans, saying, as he would write later, "to all of us that this virus of hate that has seeped into the veins of our nation, if unchecked will lead inevitably to our moral and spiritual doom." For King and for all other Americans, this day, this event, was a point of focus, a point of definition, a lull in a gathering storm. With the high and mighty, with King Baudouin, Queen Frederika, Charles de Gaulle, Haile Selassie, and other world leaders, Martin Luther King, Jr., thirty-four, a descendant of slaves, filed out of St. Matthew's Cathedral, wondering. He was convinced then and he would say later in word and deed that the most enduring monument to John F. Kennedy and all the other martyrs of this year would be an enlargement of "the sense of humanity of a whole people."

Southern Christian Leadership Conference delegates
display identifying symbols. Demonstrators covered
both sides of reflecting pool of Lincoln Monument and
stretched a mile to the east. Reporters called event "a
visible expression of interracial brotherhood" and "an
almost unprecedented exhibition of resolve."

Rabbi Joachim Prinz, president of American Jewish Congress, addresses crowd. Other speakers included Roy Wilkins, Asa Philip Randolph, John Lewis, Eugene Carson Blake, and Whitney M. Young, Jr. Marian Anderson and Mahalia Jackson were among outstanding artists who contributed time and talent to occasion.

At conclusion of March on Washington, King and
other leaders conferred with President John F. Kennedy.
The President said: "The cause of twenty million
Negroes has been advanced by the program conducted
so appropriately before the nation's shrine to the Great
Emancipator. . . ."

Climbing ladder leading to platform for television
personnel, King displays rare public beam. The five
major Negro organizations—SCLC, NAACP, SNCC,
Urban League, CORE—and church and labor groups
sponsored March which was designed to focus demands
for "Freedom and Jobs." More than 250,000 people,
some 60,000 of them white, participated in historic
event.

Hero of day, King waves to huge crowd which came from points all over America and from overseas.

King's "I Have a Dream" speech was easily highlight of day. He said it would be "fatal for the nation to overlook the urgency of the moment and to underestimate the determination of the Negro."

At height of Birmingham demonstrations, Negro protesters throng streets in front of Sixteenth Street Baptist
Church, which was focal point in King-led campaign
against city's color-caste system. Demonstrations lasted
five weeks, played key role in detonating Negro
rebellion of the summer of 1963.

Workers remove rubble after bombing of Sixteenth Street Baptist Church by segregationists. Four children were killed in September 15, 1963, bombing which shocked nation.

Young pallbearers take casket to hearse after mass funeral for victims of the bombing. King and other leaders spoke at the funeral which was held in the Sixth Street Baptist Church. King said the young victims were martyrs to the cause of freedom and justice.

Man

In a wry comment on the pains of secular canonization in the harsh glare of kleig lights, Gandhi said: "The woes of Mahatmas are known to Mahatmas only."

Martin Luther King, faced with similar problems, phrased the matter differently but no less pungently. The problem, he said, was *"the general strain of being known"*—that and the additional problem of trying "at all times to keep the gulf between the public self and private self at a minimum."

By almost all accounts, King succeeded admirably in narrowing the gulf between the private man and the public man. But his unique situation militates against an elimination of the gulf. Like all public men, King found it necessary to erect psychic windbreaks against the storm of his own public acclaim. Like all symbols, King found it necessary to be two men in order to make himself and others one.

In order to let his nerve fibers mend, King retreated from time to time into a private world that sustains and reinvigorates the inner man. The private world was surprisingly compact, embracing a small area around the Auburn Avenue of his birth. Not only King's office but also his church and, a few blocks away, his two-story red-brick home were located in the Auburn Avenue area of Atlanta. Home, office, and church, which he copastored with his father, are commodious and comfortable, nothing pretentious, nothing grand, all reflecting somehow the balance and stolidity of the man himself. Rigorously honest, ever mindful of his exposed position, King bent over backward to avoid the almost universal view that the appetites and appurtenances of Negro leaders grow with their fame. He lived simply, unostentatiously, in a big house in one of Atlanta's less fashionable Negro neighborhoods. Nothing distinguishes the King home from others in the middle-class neighborhood except the medium-weight iron bars on the window sills and the front door. This door opens into one of two large living rooms, separated by an archway, which extend across the front of the house. These rooms and others in the house have a lived-in appearance. Modestly furnished, threatened subtly by outside pressures, weighed down with books, sheet music, awards, the rooms speak of the contemplative pleasures, of words, melodies, and ideas, and of the threats to those pleasures—action, struggle, fame, pain. Entering the house, one's attention is arrested immediately by several paintings with Afro-American themes—one by the great-great granddaughter of John Brown—and a large photograph of Gandhi. Beneath these paintings, on the mantel and on a large coffee table, are mementos of King's travels, African sculpture, bric-a-brac, *objets d'art*. Nearby, on an end table, are two awards, one a bust of Franklin Delano Roosevelt. This room opens into the second, larger living room which is dominated by a grand piano. Behind this room, through another archway, is the dining room. Further back, on the same floor, is King's office-den, a gray-metal desk and double-file cabinet sitting in the middle of the floor, surrounded by a bewildering maze of boxes, cabinets and shelving containing tapes of speeches, manuscripts, books, and letters. There are also large file cabinets along the walls. One drawer in the larger cabinets holds nothing except King's earned and honorary degrees. Upstairs, on the second floor, are the children's bedrooms, one complete with a bearskin rug, and the master bedroom, dominated by a huge, king-sized bed.

King was not often in this house. Two-thirds of his time was spent elsewhere, a fact which disturbed him greatly. He had a feeling akin to guilt over his extended absences from his family. He said privately and on occasions publicly that nothing disturbed him more than his inability to fulfill his demanding concept of what the head of a household should be. To compensate for unavoidable absences on speaking trips, fund-raising campaigns, and other duties connected with the civil rights movement, he lived intensely at home, trying to cram weeks and months of missed living into a few days. He gave special attention to the four children, all of whom were born in or on the edge of a racial or a personal crisis: Yolanda Denise (Yoki), November 17, 1955; Martin Luther King III (Marty), October 23, 1957; Dexter, January 30, 1961; and Bernice Albertine (Bunny), March 28, 1963.

The prophet abroad is not honored generally in his home city, but he was a hero to his children who, Coretta King has said, "are wild about him." At least one of the children shared a widely-held public view. Marty is convinced that his father could "fix" the American racial problem single-handedly.

With Marty and the other children, King was the direct opposite of the solemn, serious prophet the world knew. Behind the door with the iron bars, King got down on the floor with his youngsters and wrestled and brawled. Sometimes he turned the living room into a handball court for himself and the young Kings. When Coretta objected, King replied, to the delight of his children: "Where else do we have to play?"

As a father, King leaned toward risky, fate-defying games. "He has a habit," Coretta has written, "which they dearly love, of letting them stand on the steps leading to the second floor and catching them as they jump down into his arms. When they were babies, he used to put them up on top of the refrigerator. They would hurl themselves into his arms without even seeming to look. I died a thousand deaths each time they played this little game. I just knew that one of those times, someone was going to get hurt. . . ."

Though a rebel, if not a revolutionary, King was far from impetuous. A curious blend of idealism and practicality, he recalled not the destructive but the constructive, traditional values. In affairs of the family, he was, in fact, a staunch conservative. His father's child, he had a strong family sense and was rigorously committed to the Puritan verities: hard work, sobriety, balance, order. And although he condemned conspicuous consumption, he said that the Biblical injunction against laying up treasures on earth was a parable that should not be taken literally. His views on marriage were predictably conventional. In an *Ebony* magazine column, "Advice for Living," King wrote: "In advising anyone on marital problems I usually begin by urging each person to do an honest job of self-analysis. . . . People fail to get along with each other because they fear each other. They fear each other because they don't know each other. They don't know each other because they have not properly communicated with each other. . . . A marriage that is based only on external beauty lacks the solid rock of permanence and stability. One must discover the meaning of soul beauty before he has really discovered the meaning of love."

King admitted, also, that passive resistance has some limitations as a parental tool. Spanking, he said, should be used in moderation "whenever necessary." But he contended, as his father contended, that modern parents would not find it necessary to resort to the rod if they would establish from the beginning the proper home atmosphere of discipline and training.

The King children were aware of their father's weight in the world— and of his woes. After his arrest in Atlanta in 1960, Yoki ran home from school, weeping. Someone, she told her mother, had said her father was in jail. Coretta, searching for words a young girl could understand said: "Your Daddy went to jail to help people. You know, some people don't have nice homes to live in, good food to eat or clothes to wear. Your Daddy is trying to make it possible for all people to have all these things." Coretta said later that she "couldn't expect them—Yoki was then four and Marty two—to think in terms of the abstract concepts of freedom, democracy or equality. I had to offer them something concrete, something simple and basic."

The words worked, apparently, for the children soon began to take pride in the idea that their father was helping other people by going to jail. Still, there were aspects of this occupation that seemed a trifle odd to the juvenile mind. And when King was arrested in Albany, Yoki, hearing the news on television, was overcome with grief. This time, to Coretta's surprise, Marty supplied the soothing words.

"Don't cry, Yoki," he said. "Daddy's gone to help more people. He's already helped some people. But he has to help some more now. When he finishes, he'll be back."

Although King tried to spend every free moment and every major holiday with the children, the burden of structuring the family's private life fell, as these incidents indicate, on the shoulders of Coretta King. A sensitive, strong-willed young woman, who would "rather be called intelligent than pretty," Coretta handled the chore with practiced aplomb. She not only mothered four children and ran a house which had become an international stopping-off place, but she also made occasional concert appearances as a soprano. Her role in the Freedom movement was an important one, not only as a buffer and booster for her husband but also as a substitute speaker and a complementary symbol. In 1962, she was one of a group of forty American women who attended a disarmament conference in Geneva. The next year, she received one of the first Louise Waterman awards of the national women's division of the American Jewish Congress.

Coretta, who is five-feet-four, big-boned and attractive, was in many ways a perfect complement to her husband. She is not by nature nonviolent. The spirit of the thing, she has said, is somewhat alien to her personality. "I was a mean, mean child," she has said. "I've had continually to talk to myself, praying out loud, asking the Lord not to let me become bitter about things. I've been helped by Martin, because his personality is so different from mine." Like Martin King, Coretta King has grown with the concept of nonviolence. Today, she is one of the more articulate exponents of the King doctrine. Totally devoted to the Freedom movement, she has also faced and transcended the possibility of death. To audiences across the country, she is fond of quoting the book of Esther: "And if I perish, I perish."

Although King delegated many family responsibilities, he found time to supervise personal details, including his wife's selection of clothes. He had strong likes and dislikes in this area, preferring his wife in wide skirts with fitted waists. He loathed chemise-type garments which, he said, are typical of "the schizophrenia of the age." "They look like one thing in front and another thing behind." King himself was an immaculate dresser, favoring three-button lounge suits in conservative colors.

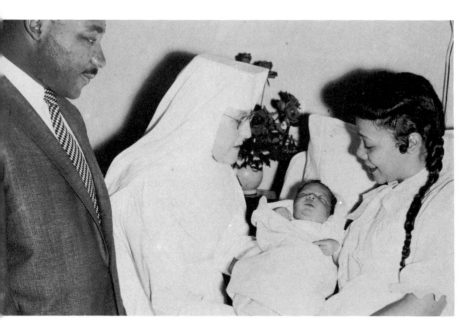

At St. Jude's Hospital in Montgomery, Sister Alexander shows new baby, Martin Luther King III, to mother and father. Baby was born on October 23, 1957, almost two years after birth of first child, Yolanda Denise.

In Montgomery, King plays with young daughter, Yolanda (Yoki), in front of Dexter Avenue Baptist Church. He has strong sense of family and of parental responsibilities.

In rare informal pose, taken in 1957, King and wife
push Yolanda's stroller on sidewalk near their
Montgomery home. Kings now have four children.

He was fond of sports clothes but seldom wore them in public, a fact which indicated, to his wife at any rate, "that deep down he wants to be casual, but can never do it."

Time permitting, King and his wife enjoyed vibrant social activities with a close circle of friends. Both, however, avoided the intense, brittle social round that passes for society. As a public figure, however, King attended occasional cocktail parties but limited himself to non-alcoholic drinks. He said that it is "almost impossible for business and professional people to avoid being invited to cocktail parties on some occasions. . . . However, it is possible to attend a cocktail party and not participate in the drinking activities."

Despite his international fame, King suffered the same disabilities as other Atlanta Negroes. Twice since 1960, he attempted to enroll his children in a private (white) Episcopal school near his home; and twice the children were rejected on racial grounds. After the second incident, an anonymous white Atlantan made an interesting observation. Said he: "It gives one pause to realize that Atlanta may be chiefly remembered as the birthplace of Coca-Cola and Martin Luther King and that contemporary Atlantans do not seem to realize it."

In Atlanta, King rose early and read for thirty minutes or so before breakfast. On rare holidays, he padded about the house, playing with the children, listening to operatic records, reading, or tinkering with the piano. "He starts off Moonlight Sonata," Coretta said, "as if you're really going to hear something, but he fades out." King also liked to cook, but his schedule left little time for that diversion. There was even less time for the baseball, football and, paradoxically, boxing he once followed closely. His chief diversion now was music, especially opera.

No ascetic, King had a balanced appreciation for the sensuous pleasures of life. He was a hearty eater, with a particular fondness for steak and ethnic delicacies, black-eyed peas, collard greens, barbecue. Coretta recalled that on New York visits it has been necessary to make a special trip to Harlem for barbecue. "Eating," King said, "is my great sin." He has also expressed some contempt for modern women "who want to get married and can't cook a lick."

Because of the nature of his occupation, King's at-home schedule had no particular texture or consistency. His father relieved him of most pastoral duties, though King tried to preach at least one or two sermons at Ebenezer each month. Far more time consuming, however, was his work at the Southern Christian Leadership Conference. On most working days, King went to the SCLC offices on the first floor of the Negro Masonic Temple, a block away from the church. King's office was large and spacious but hardly what the average person would associate with a man of such eminence. The office floor is a polished hardwood that has been called "golden oak." A row of shelves on the pale green walls housed King's books in several translations and philosophical and religious publications. Another set of shelves held photographs of his wife and children. King's desk was a working man's desk, spare, functional. Nothing in the room indicated the weight of the man except the two telephones, one with the SCLC number, the other bearing a conspicuously blank piece of paper.

From this room and over these two telephones, especially the unlisted one, Martin Luther King the private man communed with and made articulate to himself and to others the public man. SCLC, the instrument rather than the base of his power, is an organization of organizations composed of some one hundred church-oriented groups in the South. Under King's leadership, SCLC grew from a nucleate of five people with a budget of $63,000 in 1960 to a 1963 staff of forty and a budget of $800,000.

It is a matter of some moment that SCLC is a Southern, not a national, organization. This fact posed large problems for King, who was a national, if not an international leader. Broadly stated, the central problem was that King had national responsibility without a validating instrument of national power. In a sense, King was a victim of his own structural dilemma. He decided, as we have seen, in 1957 that he was a *Southern* Negro leader. Though men urged him to seek national leadership, King decided against such a move, limiting himself, *as a matter of policy*, to the South. Men close to him have suggested that he did not want to offend the NAACP and the Negro leadership structure by invading the North. Whatever the reason, King's decision to make SCLC a Southwide rather than a nationwide organization severely limited his leadership as distinguished from his unprecedented influence. King later remedied this structural defeat by invading Chicago and other cities and by opening offices in Northern centers.

King and SCLC were involved in a number of programs (voter registration, leadership training, etc.) but their foremost emphasis, as King said, was "to spread the philosophy of nonviolence and to demonstrate through action its operational techniques." Though the details of these operations are handled by other men, King maintained firm central control. When he was out of town, he was in contact with Dora MacDonald, his tall, pretty and efficient secretary, at least once and sometimes two or three times a day. To an extent unprecedented in the civil rights field, King was the organization he headed. Despite that fact, he refused to accept a salary from the organization. He was paid $1.00 a year by SCLC and $6,000 annually by Ebenezer Baptist Church. The bulk of his income came from speaking engagements, royalties, and magazine articles.

As a leader, King recalled not Gandhi but Franklin Delano Roosevelt. Like Roosevelt, he tended to dawdle, to procrastinate, waiting for events to coagulate and for God to show him the right way. In moments of great crisis, he decided almost always through prayer, which is another way of saying that he decided also through a communion with his subconscious. There was an incident in the Birmingham crisis that reveals, in a brief, illuminating flash, King's decision-making processes. The movement at the time was on the verge of collapse for lack of bail bond money. As it happened, King was scheduled to go to jail at that precise moment. Since he was more valuable out of jail than in jail, his aides pleaded with him to delay the step. King listened to all sides and then withdrew to another room to think, to meditate, to pray. He returned a few minutes later and announced that he was going to jail. "I don't know what will happen," he said. "I don't know where the money will come from. But I have to make a faith act." The next day, God or fate provided the bail money—through Harry Belafonte. This development, of course, reaffirmed King's belief that "God's companionship does not stop at the door of a jail cell." Although King's decision-making methods have proved apt to his purposes, they have not contributed to the peace of mind of associates who live in a somewhat more distant relation to divinity.

There are other similarities to the Roosevelt leadership syndrome. King, like Roosevelt, had an unexcelled ability to make ideas live. Like Roosevelt, he was more a shaper of action than a maker of action, more a broker of ideas than a creator of ideas. As a nonviolent tactician and thinker, he was not noticeably superior to James Farmer or Bayard Rustin, or to his associates, Wyatt Tee Walker and James Lawson. Unlike these men, however, King could take an idea and put flesh and bone on it. Like Gandhi, like Roosevelt, like all great leaders, he had an instinct for symbolic action: he could dramatize an idea in action.

Another trait of the public man, revelative of the inner man, was his ability to relax in transit. In repose, he released his body, shooting his legs out, resting his feet on chairs, desks, and sofas. Another restorative was a fifteen- or thirty-minute nap in the middle of the day or the middle of a crisis. As a result of these techniques of self-preservation, King was capable of considerable concentration and lengthy expenditures of energy over long periods. In fact, he often went for extended periods with as little as four hours' sleep a night. During the Birmingham struggle, he was awake and active for almost three days at a stretch.

Between big events, between Albanys and Birminghams, King's world was a world of airplanes, hotels, kleig lights, banquet tables, and lecture platforms. In an almost nonstop performance, he traveled from three to four thousand miles a week, explaining his philosophy to students, Presidents, white liberals, Negro militants, maids, millionaires, and moderates. Though a private citizen, King usually received the honors (police guards, police motorcades, sirens, etc.) of visiting royalty. In one twenty-four-hour visit to a major city, he usually managed two or three formal speeches, a press conference, and several interviews with radio, television, and print media personnel.

In speeches and interviews, King dwelled almost always on four major themes: 1) nonviolence, 2) social change, 3) individual and collective responsibility, and 4) the price of freedom. Increasingly, in recent years, he has also stressed nonracial themes, particularly the inequitable distribution of wealth and the threat of a nuclear war. Although he backed pacifist postures, King said he was "no doctrinaire pacifist." He saw the pacifist position "not as sinless but as the lesser evil." ". . . I am convinced," he wrote, "that the church cannot remain silent while mankind faces the threat of being plunged into the abyss

In Montgomery home in 1957, King and wife watch
Yolanda demonstrate her proficiency with the hoola-
hoop. King is holding son, Martin III. He was overjoyed by birth of son, said: "When you live close to
the Lord, you get what you order."

In Atlanta home in 1963, Coretta Scott King poses with
children: Bernice, Yolanda, Martin III, and Dexter.
Burden of organizing family's private life
falls on shoulders of Coretta King who is also a
concert singer.

King is greeted by wife and children after his release
from Reidsville State Prison in October, 1960. Children
visited King in August, 1962, in Albany, Georgia, jail.

of nuclear annihilation. If the church is true to its mission it must call for an end to the arms race."

Unlike some Negro leaders, King used the same speech before white audiences and Negro audiences. He did find it necessary on occasions, however to remind Negroes that God helps those who help themselves. King realized that segregationists and some liberals use this same argument to justify segregation, but he said that Negro leadership must take the risk of being misunderstood in a massive crusade to raise standards in the ghetto. In interviews and speeches, King made three points:

> 1. We [Negroes] depend too much on white philanthropy. Too often those of us who are in the middle class live above our means, spend money on nonessentials and fail to lend financial support to organizations and educational institutions which so desperately need funds.

> 2. We are often too loud and boisterous, and spend too much on alcoholic beverages. These are some of the shortcomings we can improve here and now. . . . Even the most poverty stricken among us can be clean, even the most uneducated among us can have high morals. By improving these standards, we will go a long way in breaking down some of the arguments of the segregationists.

> 3. In other words, we must work on two fronts. On the one hand we must continually resist the system of segregation—the system which is the basic cause of our lagging standards; on the other hand we must work constructively to improve the lagging standards which are the effects of segregation. There must be a rhythm of alternation between attacking the cause and healing the effects.

Although King spared no one, he was fervently received by audiences of from ten to two hundred thousand. His appeal was diffuse, chaotic, complex. Not only Negro Americans but a large number of white Americans looked to him for leadership and an articulation of their yearnings. Most Negroes, of course, saw in King a hope, a promise, and perhaps an opportunity to evade their own responsibilities. Many elderly Negro women, moreover, had an almost religious reverence for the young Baptist minister, seeing in him the son they wished for or the man they had hoped their husbands would be. We are on shakier grounds when we ask ourselves what white Americans saw in King. He had, of course, an appeal akin to Kennedy's, the call of youth to youth and of idealism to idealism. He also touched the silent music of a Christianity made mute by materialism and gadgetry. It is also highly probable that many white Americans were fascinated by the word "love" in the romantic sense and the never-dying American hope that errors committed will not have to be paid for.

King explained repeatedly that he came "not to bring peace, but a sword," a "sword that heals," to be sure, but nevertheless a sword. He tried also to tell his audiences that the love of which he spoke is a love that has never been sung and very seldom honored. "When we talk about love at this point we are not talking about emotional bosh or sentimental affection. It's nonsense to tell an oppressed people to love their oppressors in an affectional sense. . . ." Also, in a little-noted statement, King said "we may have to repent in this generation not merely for the vitriolic actions and words of the bad people, but also for the appalling silence and apathy of the good people."

It would seem, however, that what King said was not nearly as important as how he said it. He was a speaker with deep roots in the Negro religious tradition of resounding, repetitive rhetoric. He spoke mostly without notes, often repeating speeches he had given elsewhere. What he lost in the process—a clarification and development of his ideas in transit—he gained in immediacy and fervency of responses. King seldom moved from the spot where he planted himself. He used few gestures but when he gestured the movement almost always complemented the word. He relied almost totally on his voice, a deep and throaty baritone. The range of the voice was not impressive, but King used it well, pacing himself in a near-conversational tone, alternating quiet passages with expansive rhythmic sections, building to a climax in a crescendo of staccato phrases. Like almost all great Negro preachers, like almost all great Negro singers, King attacked key phrases, hanging them up in the audience's mind, "worrying them," as the blues singers say, his voice trembling and rising in anger, in indignation, in wrath. King also knew the value of understatement. He seemed always to be holding something in reserve. He gave the impression of a man who could say more, tell more, reveal more, in another setting. On the debit side, it should be said that King had a fondness for polarities (black-white, thick-thin, mountain-valley) and for alliterative devices that please the ear and sometimes offend the eye.

King was a great speaker, however, not because of his technique or his lack of technique. As Ralph Waldo Emerson pointed out one hundred years ago, "There has to be a man behind the speech." King's greatness as a public speaker and as a public man grew out of, was a reflection of, the resolved tensions of the inner man.

At five-feet-seven, a trifle pudgy from years at the banquet table, the man was not an overwhelmingly imposing figure. Yet, there was about him a quiet strength, a troubled calmness, that pulled people to him and bound them to his words and deeds. Men and women vied with each other in describing this elusive quality. They have named it inner contentment, ego-security, naturalness. It seemed to Donald M. Schwartz, a Chicago reporter, that King, the Baptist minister, was "what jazz musicians call 'loose' (meaning relaxed), even in a precisely pressed dark blue suit and a sparkling white shirt." Coretta King has called attention to this same quality. "There is something in his manner that is easy. He is easy to know, very friendly. He makes people feel a sense of their own worth by not asserting himself. If you didn't know who he was nothing would distinguish him from anybody else." She added, however: "Of course, he has the utmost confidence in himself, though he never gives that impression."

Coretta King's analysis reminds us anew that King was infinitely more complex than is generally assumed. That complexity was masked, not revealed, by his great skill in the politics of personality, a skill rooted in the heritage of the Baptist preacher. There is truth in the assertion that King possessed a Gandhi-like center of calm; but there is truth also in the assertion that King, like John F. Kennedy, was almost perpetually detached, suspended somewhere, as he has said, between the natural extrovert and the indrawn introvert. Though he gave the impression of great warmth, he was not very outgoing in public. There is about him what Claude Sitton of the New York Times called "a pensive detachment." But his detachment, as James Baldwin noted, "is not, on the other hand, of that icily uneasy, nerve-racking kind to be encountered in so many famous Negroes who have allowed their aspirations and notoriety to destroy their identities and who always seem to be giving an uncertain imitation of some extremely improbable white man."

There was in King also a deep strain of mysticism. He was not often ill, but when illness overtook him "he has wondered," biographer Reddick wrote, "if he would pull through." Flowing with and out of this was a strong sense of fate. He gave the impression of a man driven by some overpowering force. Almost all of his statements on himself were tinged with the distantly negative sense of a man gripped, possessed, by God or fate or history. Consider, for example, the following statement: "History has thrust me into this position. It would be both immoral and a sign of ingratitude if I did not face my moral responsibility to do what I can in this struggle."

One final fact in the complicated personal equation of Martin Luther King, Jr.,was that an air of incipient martyrdom, of precariousness and fragility, hung over him. He seemed somehow threatened, menaced. The air of danger was not delusive. Repeated attempts were made on his life and he received daily threats.

All these currents bubbled beneath the surface of the public and private man. What gave King his "efficient grace," what annealed the public and the private man, was the subordination and transcendence of all these strains in the seizure and service of a consuming ideal. His, in sum, was the simplicity of a resolved, an integrated complexity.

Presence

By the end of the centennial celebration of the Emancipation Proclamation, Martin Luther King, Jr. was more than a symbol. His influence, running on before him, shooting off sparks, had made him a presence in the land, a pervasive and prevailing social force. By that time, he was the leader not only of millions of Negroes but also of hundreds of thousands of whites. Wherever race was spoken of, in this season—and it was spoken of almost everywhere—there also King was spoken of. It was in relation to him or in opposition to him that men defined themselves and their racial postures.

Seeing these things in him, and others, Lyndon Baines Johnson, the new President, summoned him almost immediately to the White House to confer on the change of administration. The two Southerners got on famously. Johnson's approach to the racial problem, King wrote later, "was not identical with mine—nor had I expected it to be.

197

Yet his careful practicability was nonetheless clearly no mask to conceal indifference. His emotional and intellectual involvement were genuine and devoid of adornment. It was conspicuous that he was searching for a solution to a problem he knew to be a major shortcoming in American life. I came away strengthened in my conviction that an undifferentiated approach to white Southerners could be a grave error, all too easy for Negro leaders in the heat of bitterness." King pledged the new President his support and good will in the difficult period of transition. But he told him, significantly, that there would be no cooling-off period and that demonstrations would resume after the period of national mourning.

There were two other tokens in this period of the pervasive influence of the King *mystique*. The first was selection of King as "Man of the Year" by *Time*, the weekly news magazine. No other Negro, except Haile Selassie, had been so honored since the institution of the category in 1927, two years before King's birth. *Time* said King was selected "as a man—but also as the representative of his people, for whom 1963 was perhaps the most important year in their history." The American Negro, the magazine said, "made 1963 the year of his outcry for equality, of massive demonstrations, of sit-ins and speeches and street fighting, of soul searching in the suburbs and psalm singing in the jails." Birmingham, *Time* continued, was the main battleground of the "Negro Revolution," "and Martin Luther King, Jr., the leader of the Negroes in Birmingham, became to millions, black and white, in South and North, the symbol of the revolution—and the Man of the Year." King said, characteristically, that he considered the honor as "not a personal tribute, but a tribute to the whole freedom movement and the people who participated and continue to participate."

Another token, even more unprecedented, was the nomination of King by eight members of the Swedish Parliament as a candidate for the 1964 Nobel Peace Prize. *Swedish officials said King was nominated because he "had succeeded in keeping his followers to the principle of nonviolence." They added: "Without King's confirmed

*A committee composed of five members of the Norwegian parliament selects the winner of the Nobel Peace Prize. Nominations are made by qualified persons in all parts of world.

effectiveness . . . demonstrations and marches could easily have become violent and ended with the spilling of blood." Though pleased, King did not give the matter a great deal of attention. He thought it very unlikely that he, a private citizen, would be chosen for the world's most prestigious award out of a field reported to include French President Charles de Gaulle, former President Dwight David Eisenhower, former West German Chancellor Konrad Adenauer and Lord Avon, the former British Prime Minister Sir Anthony Eden.

Far more important to King at the moment was the American racial problem, which was growing more complex by the hour. Analyzing the situation in his annual "progress report" for *Nation* magazine, King said that "Negro power had matured and was dynamically asserting itself." Nothing, he believed, in Negro history, except the Reconstruction era, equalled "in intensity, breadth and power" the "matchless upheaval" of 1963. It was time now, he concluded, for the federal government "to muster enough courage and determination" to aid Negro demonstrators. King called specifically for "creative innovations," the assignment, for example, of federal marshals in situations unsuitable for federal troops.

What of the Freedom movement?

What turn would the struggle take in the months ahead?

King told United Press International that the massive demonstration phase of the campaign was "about over." The big push of the year, he said, would be to "transform the moral offensive that was mobilized last year into political power this year." He also raised the possibility of a nationwide "selective buying" campaign. King admitted that the Freedom movement was somewhat in the doldrums but said this was "the inevitable pause that takes place in any movement to assess your gains, to determine your future course and to put yourself in a better position for larger leaps."

King was necessarily vague about the nature of the leap, for he was under increasing pressure at that juncture from two separate groups: Negro moderates and militants who wanted to de-escalate the growing crisis and Negro activists who were saying King's philosophy of nonviolence was "too slow" and "too conciliatory." Biding his time, threading his way through bitterly-divided leadership groups, King picked St. Augustine, Florida, as the focal point of his spring and summer campaign. St. Augustine, America's oldest city, had several

After post-assassination meeting with new President, Lyndon B. Johnson, King holds White House press conference. He pledged support to Administration in difficult transition period but said demonstrations would resume after the period of national mourning.

With other national leaders, King confers with President Johnson on civil rights legislation and the projected "war on poverty." Also pictured, from left, are: Roy Wilkins, executive director of NAACP; James Farmer, national director of CORE; Whitney M. Young, Jr., executive director, National Urban League.

At White House ceremony marking passage of historic
Civil Rights Bill, King and other leaders receive pens
President Johnson used to sign legislation. Bill, which
late President Kennedy submitted to Congress after
Birmingham demonstrations, was passed on July 2, 1964.

advantages. First, it was almost totally segregated. Second, the city had great symbolic value because of the approaching celebration of its four-hundredth anniversary. Third, SCLC had strong local connections in the town. For these reasons and others, St. Augustine became a King-designated center of the Freedom movement struggle. The campaign began at Easter with skirmishes and reconnaisances and reached a peak in May and June. During these months, there were a series of night mass marches through the old slave market in the town square.

In previous campaigns, King had been opposed mainly by local police officials. But St. Augustine presented an entirely different picture. With police officials offering only token opposition, King's forces were battered nightly by local rowdies brandishing chains, clubs, and vials of sulphuric acid. King appealed to the President, saying St. Augustine was "the most lawless community" he had ever encountered. He insisted, however, that there would be no turning back. "We are determined," he told a mass meeting, "[that] this city will not celebrate its quadricentennial as a segregated city. There will be no turning back."

To emphasize this point, King announced his determination to seek his twelfth jail sentence. On June 11, with Ralph Abernathy and a party of sixteen, he staged a stand-in at an exclusive restaurant overlooking Matanzas Bay. The twenty-minute confrontation between King and restaurant owner James Brock was one of those little vignettes that etches swiftly and unforgettably the spirit and sweep of a whole epoch. King and Brock stood three feet apart and talked. Neither man raised his voice or said a word in anger. This was the dialogue:

> King: I and my friends have come to lunch.
> Brock: We can't serve you. We are not integrated.
> King: We'll wait around. We feel you should serve us.
> Brock: You are on private property. We reserve the right to refuse service. I ask you on behalf of myself, my wife and my children to leave.

King: We are sorry you have that attitude. You are doing a dis-service to the nation.

Brock: You can't push this thing. We are a small business. We are caught in the middle of something. We find ourselves between two armed camps. If we integrate now it would hurt our business.

King: We will stand here and hope that in the process that our conscious efforts will make this a better land.

Brock: We will integrate under one of two conditions, by feder-al court order or if a responsible group of citizens ask us to open to all customers.

King: We are glad to know that you would do it under those conditions.

Abernathy: Does your invitation to serve tourists include Ne-groes?

Brock: Negroes can only be served in the service area of the res-taurant. Maids and chauffeurs of white visitors have been served that way in the past.

King: Can't you see how this humiliates us?

Brock: Will you please take your nonviolent army somewhere else? I must remind you that I have already had eighty-five people arrested before at my place.

(Police Chief Virgil Stuart arrived.)

Brock to Stuart: "I'm glad you are here. I have explained to Dr. King that we cannot serve them. I have asked Dr. King to leave twice, but he has refused."

Stuart to King's party: "You are all under arrest."

King and his companions were booked on charges of violating Flori-da's "unwanted guest law." King remained in prison for two days and was then released on $900 bail. What happened next was as significant in its way as the restaurant confrontation. King went from jail to a pre-vious engagement at Yale University in New Haven. On Monday, June 15, he and twelve other distinguished Americans received honorary de-grees at the university's 263rd commencement. King was cited for an "eloquence that has kindled the nation's sense of outrage" and for hav-ing displayed a "steadfast refusal to countenance violence." President Kingman Brewster, Jr., read the citation:

Focal point of King-led demonstrations in St. Augustine, Florida, was old slave market in town square. Demonstrations reached peak in May and June, 1964.

Pickets stage sympathy march in support of St. Augustine demonstrations which focused national spotlight on city on eve of its quadricentennial celebration. Negro demonstrators were attacked with bricks, bottles, sticks, firecrackers.

Dive-in at Monson Motor Lodge is halted by manager James Brock who emptied contents of jug labeled "muriatic acid" into motel swimming pool as Negro and white demonstrators screamed.

King and Ralph Abernathy are photographed in St. John's County jail after their arrest on trespassing charges at Monson Motor Lodge. King said: "This is one of the nicest jails I've been in."

When outrage and shame together shall one day have vindicated the promise of legal, social and economic opportunity for all citizens, the gratitude of peoples everywhere and of generations of Americans yet unborn will echo our admiration.

As two university marshals placed a blue and white hood over King's head, the ten thousand spectators came to their feet in a standing ovation.

This, though encouraging, did not change the situation in St. Augustine, to which King returned almost immediately. Under his direction, the campaign rose in a wave of white violence and nonviolent resistance and suffering on the part of the Negro demonstrators. Finally, on June 30, a Birmingham-type agreement was effected and King announced, somewhat prematurely, "victory." After five days of indifferent compliance with the new Civil Rights Bill, St. Augustine restaurant and hotel owners retreated under heavy pressure from white terrorists.

King's distress over this development was balanced by the encouraging response to the new Civil Rights Bill which he correctly called "a child of storm, the product of the most turbulent motion the nation had ever known in peacetime." The bill, which had been sent to Congress by John F. Kennedy after the turbulent Birmingham demonstrations, was passed on July 2, 1964.

As one of the architects of the most comprehensive legislation of its kind passed since the Reconstruction era, King was one of several leaders who witnessed the signing of the bill. King said then and later that he saw the bill as a token of the "good faith" effort he considered necessary for the maintenance of social peace in America.

Time and time again, King had warned that "nonviolence [could] not exist in a vacuum." As early as 1961, he had said: "If something isn't done in a hurry and in a vigorous way, explosive situations will develop, particularly in the large industrial areas of the North, where you have great numbers of Negroes with these frustrations emerging." As the hot weeks of the summer of 1964 wore on, the submerged frustrations King feared bubbled to the surface.

Whatever its virtues, nonviolence is a hard program to sell. After decades of agitation, Gandhi admitted, with some exaggeration, that he was perhaps the only real Gandhian in India. It began to dawn on King in this fateful summer that his support on the issue of non-violence as a way of life was hardly more substantial.

Criticism of King, which had been rising now for a year, centered in four groups: 1) the Negro power structure which contended generally that Negroes had made their point and should now retreat to the old islands of litigation and protest; 2) activists and Northern Negro intellectuals who called for a lurch forward into open civil disobedience; 3) some members and leaders of the Freedom movement who believed in nonviolence as an offensive tactic but questioned its value as a religious dogma; 4) black nationalists who said and apparently believed that King was an agent or, at least, a tool of the white power structure.

Few if any Negroes articulated a meaningful alternative to non-violence as an offensive tactic. But many Negroes, including a surprisingly large number of the Negro leadership group, championed what they called "the inalienable Western right of self-defense." Some of this, to be sure, was displaced envy, a masked attack on King and not his program. But some of the critics raised large questions about the philosophical and strategical scaffolding of the nonviolent ethic. In an interview with Robert S. Bird, the New York Herald Tribune reporter, Dr. Kenneth B. Clark, the psychologist, praised King as a leader, but said his "philosophy of love of the oppressor" was "psychologically unrealistic" and "guilt-producing" and "too close to the stereotype of the Negro for comfort, really." Taking a similar stance, novelist John O. Killens said in several public addresses and interviews: "The Negro has always been nonviolent—by necessity. I see no reason now to make a philosophy out of it."

Equally pointed were criticisms of King through Gandhi. In a New York Times magazine article, "Gandhiism Is Not Easily Copied," Ved Mehta, an Indian intellectual, said King's purposes would be better served by an adoption of Gandhi's tactics and a rejection of Gandhi's theories which, Mehta said, "leave a lot to be explained and vindicated." Mehta added: "Contrary to what is sometimes thought, most of Gandhi's magic was in his actions. . . . His life was crowded with a

Negro and white citizens, ministers, rabbis, priests, and nuns attended the rally which was called to demonstrate broad interracial and interfaith support for the basic goals of the Freedom movement. Rev. Theodore Hesburgh, president of Notre Dame University, also addressed the crowd.

Framed by huge columns, part of crowd of seventy-five thousand
listen to King address at June, 1964, civil rights rally in
Soldier Field, Chicago. Rally was organized by interfaith,
interracial, citizens group. Other speakers included James Farmer
of CORE, James Forman of SNCC.

Addressing rally, King calls for a continuation of freedom struggle. Speaking
extemporaneously, he also stressed the
need for a massive attack on what he
called the "undesirable" social effects
of discrimination.

succession of Boston Tea Parties. And, theory or no, Dr. King and his people have demonstrated how a strike here, a sit-in there, a ride here, can revolutionize race relations. Their demonstration, as was Gandhi's, is not like that of a mathematical theorem but an artistic performance. Thus, ultimately, the life-blood of the nonviolence movement may not be theology, politics, or even economics, but only art."

Similar questions about the Gandhian base were raised at a Conference on Nonviolence and Social Change which was held at Howard University in November, 1963. Several experts at this conference expressed the guarded view that the magic of nonviolence probably lay in "the economic pressure of strikes, boycotts, and the discouragement of new investments in an area because of the threat of civil disorder. . . ." Dr. Jerome D. Frank, a professor of psychiatry at Johns Hopkins University, went on to express other reservations. So far, he said, "only groups that believe that they cannot hope to win by violence have adhered to nonviolent tactics. . . . Furthermore, these nonviolent movements could potentially mobilize superior violence on their side. The British knew that too harsh suppression of Gandhi and his followers would stimulate violent revolutionary movements, and they were fighting for their existence at the time. . . . In our country, the federal courts can mobilize overwhelming power in defense of Negro rights as Mississippi has learned, and Martin Luther King has wondered in print whether the Montgomery bus strike could have succeeded if the Supreme Court decision had not come through in the nick of time."

"Moreover," Dr. Frank continued, "leaders of nonviolent movements constantly remind their opponents that if their demands are not met, they may not be able to keep their followers in check. Is the threat of violence an integral part of the success of nonviolence? Can nonviolent campaigns succeed in the complete absence of this threat? If not, are they truly nonviolent?"

Most importantly, Dr. Frank posed the question: "What do nonviolent fighters do with their impulses to violence? The continual humiliations and threats to which they are exposed must arouse intense anger which they must repress. Psychiatrists believe from clinical experience that emotions that are blocked from direct expression tend to manifest themselves obliquely. . . . " In stressing these "doubts," Dr. Frank warned against expecting "more of nonviolent methods of fighting than of violent ones. No form of waging conflict always wins. The most one can ask for nonviolent techniques is that where they fail, and they certainly will fail sometimes, violent methods would have failed more completely."

Public criticism of King, to the extent that it was confined to intellectuals, was not urgently important. In a sense, the internal ferment represented the growing pains of a new movement. Moreover, intellectuals, Negro or white, were not likely to start a riot or to join one. Very different was the case in the depths of the ghetto where men, as Howard Thurman has said, live in a primary relation with violence and with death. The burden of the color-caste system fell on the depressed strata in the big ghettos of the North. And the burden of proof was on King and America to prove to the truly disinherited that nonviolence produced palpable results.

King was realistic enough to concede that nonviolence had to win victories in order to win converts. He was, therefore, discomfited by the tide of reaction that rolled over America in the spring of 1964. By that time, demonstrations had reached what seemed to be a point of diminishing return. Southerners were easily crushing demonstrations by massive repression. Worse, demonstrations, North and South, had not succeeded in winning basic concessions. As a result, voices of despair grew louder. Events in the summer of 1964 turned the scattered voices into a swelling chorus of dissent. First, there were widely-disseminated scenes of white terrorists whacking St. Augustine demonstrators with chains and sticks. Second, and more important, there was the traumatic shock that followed the assassination of three students—two white and one Negro—involved in the Mississippi summer project.

To make matters worse, misery was deepening in the North. The Civil Rights Bill, with sections on fair employment and public accommodations, was a giant step forward, but it did not begin to touch the edges of the problem. Negro unemployment was still at a 1930 depression level in the summer of 1964. Jim Crow was still king in Birmingham and New York City, King and Gandhi and Kennedy to the contrary notwithstanding. The annual defeat of the "revenue man"; the monthly defeat of the finance company; the weekly defeat of the butcher and baker and pawnbroker; the day-by-day defeats of crumbling walls, bad plumbing, rats, roaches, and nameless bugs: these things had bred despair, desperation, and defiance. By July 18, the "vials of wrath," in Churchill's phrase, "were full" in the Harlems of America.

Bell from burned Mississippi church was exhibited at Democratic National Convention in Atlantic City. Demonstrators also focused attention on the murder of three civil rights workers in Mississippi.

Supporting interracial Mississippi Freedom Democratic party, King appears before credentials committee of Democratic National Convention on crutches. He had sprained ankle in fall.

With Rita Schwerner, wife of murdered civil rights worker, King listens to testimony before credentials committee. Witnesses said Negroes were fired from jobs, beaten and even killed for attempting to register in Mississippi. Credentials committee devised compromise which was rejected by lily-white and interracial Mississippi parties.

The grand outcome was a flash fire of riots which began in the Negro sections of New York City and leaped across the country (Rochester; Jersey City; Dixmoor, Illinois; Philadelphia). King spoke out immediately against "these outbreaks of violence." "Lawlessness, looting and violence," he said, "cannot be condoned whether used by the racist or the reckless of any color." As the nation's outstanding advocate of nonviolence, King was invited to New York City for a marathon round of discussions with Mayor Robert F. Wagner. The mayor praised King as "a truly impressive American, a figure of deep spiritual insights and great world stature," but he declined to accept King's principal recommendation, the creation of a civilian board to review charges of police brutality. King was severely criticized for his mediating efforts in the New York dispute. Even some of his friends said he was being "used" by the white power structure. More concretely, some of his aides admitted privately that it was a tactical faux pas to go into the New York dispute without a prior consultation with local Negro leaders and without some kind of prior commitment from the mayor.

However that may be, it seems likely that King's attempts to pour oil on troubled water not only in New York City but in other urban centers prevented a widening of the disturbances. The 1964 rioting, though virulent and potentially disastrous, never quite reached the scale of the 1919 and 1943 riot seasons. This would seem to indicate that King's seven-year missionary effort had at least seeded doubts in the Negro community about the wisdom of violence.

The riot season of 1964 convinced King of the necessity for a deeper involvement of all Negroes in the philosophy of nonviolence and of the further necessity for an expansion of his organizational activities. He was convinced additionally of the need for "good faith efforts" that would meet nonviolence halfway. In the SCLC Newsletter of July-August, he wrote:

> As long as thousands of Negroes in Harlem and all the little Harlems of our nation are hovered up in odorous, rat-infested ghettos; as long as the Negro finds himself smothering in an airtight cage of poverty in the midst of an affluent society; as long as the Negro feels like an exile in his own land, and sees his plight as

a long desolate corridor with no exit sign; as long as he has to attend woefully sub-standard schools and use grossly inadequate recreational facilities; as long as the Negro is daily victimized with dehumanizing squalor and depressing congestion; as long as the Negro finds his flight toward freedom constantly delayed by strong head winds of tokenism and small handouts by the white power structure, there will be an ever-present threat of violence and rioting.

In short, it is necessary to be as concerned about getting rid of the environmental conditions that caused the riots as it is to condemn the violence. To deal merely with effects and not with causes will be socially and morally suicidal. Until the Harlems and racial ghettos of our nation are destroyed and the Negro is brought into the mainstream of American life, our beloved nation will be on the verge of being plunged into the abyss of social disruption. No greater tragedy can befall a nation than to leave millions of people with a feeling that they have no stake in their society.

King spent the remaining months of the summer in exercises designed to create nonviolent men and a climate in which they could thrive. Of necessity, in the second instance, he operated primarily in the political arena. With SCLC aides, he made a "people-to-people" tour of Black Belt areas of Mississippi, urging residents to support the "Mississippi Project," a saturation voter registration effort by hundreds of Negro and white students, and the Freedom Democratic party, an integrated group which attempted unsuccessfully to unseat the lily-white Mississippi delegation to the Democratic National Convention.

King also testified before the platform committees of the Democratic and Republican conventions. At the San Francisco convention of the Republican party, he recommended a three-point program: 1) endorsement of the Civil Rights Bill, 2) condemnation of police brutality and official harassment of demonstrators, and 3) a positive program to deal with automation and unemployment. The next month, in August, he appeared before the platform committee of the Democratic National Convention with essentially the same program,

Barnstorming in North for Democratic party, King draws crowd of young admirers at nonpolitical appearance at Banneker Elementary School. He urged youth to prepare themselves for the challenges of an integrated society.

Mobbed by admirers, King pushes his way through Chicago Southside crowd. He made appearances in several Northern cities, urged Negroes to shun candidacy of Republican Senator Barry Goldwater.

Addressing rally at 47th and South Park in heart of Chicago ghetto, King says "Goldwaterism" is a threat to the free institutions of America. That night, he received the John F. Kennedy award of the Catholic Interracial Council of Chicago.

which revolved around a "Bill of Rights for the Disadvantaged." This recommendation, which became a central part of his evolving political program, called for the creation of a federal program similar to the GI Bill of Rights for veterans. In the World War II bill, King said, the nation endorsed the principle of compensating the veteran for time "lost in school or in his career or in business." The same principle, he added, should be applied to the Negro.

Certainly the Negro has been deprived. Few people consider the fact that, in addition to being enslaved for two centuries, the Negro was, during all these years, robbed of the wages of his toil. No amount of gold could provide an adequate compensation for the exploitation and humiliation of the Negro in America down through the centuries. Not all the wealth of this affluent society could meet the bill. Yet, a price can be placed on unpaid wages. The ancient common law has always provided a remedy for the appropriation of the labor of one human being by another. This law should be made to apply for American Negroes. The payment should be in the form of a massive program by the government of special, compensatory measures which could be regarded as a settlement in accordance with the accepted practice of common law. Such measures would certainly be less expensive than any computation based on *two centuries of unpaid wages* and accumulated interest.

I am proposing, therefore, that, just as we granted a GI Bill of Rights to war veterans, Americans launch a broad-based and gigantic *Bill of Rights for the Disadvantaged*, our veterans of the long seige of denial. I am specifically proposing that the platform of [this] party include an endorsement and support for the broad plan of such a Bill.

A *Bill of Rights for the Disadvantaged* would immediately transform the conditions of Negro life. The most profound alteration would not reside so much in the specific grants as in the basic psychological and motivational transformation of the Negro. I would challenge skeptics to give such a bold new approach a test for the next decade. I contend that the decline in school dropouts, family breakups, crime rates, illegitimacy, swollen relief rolls and other social evils would stagger the imagination. Change in human psychology is normally a slow process, but it is safe to predict that, when a people is ready for change as the Negro has shown himself ready today, the response is bound to be rapid and constructive.

After the nomination of Senator Barry Goldwater (R., Arizona) by the Republicans, King reassessed his political posture and decided that the time had come for a direct plunge into the political arena. He had long harbored large doubts about the wisdom of a civil rights leader taking an active role in a political campaign. But Senator Goldwater's candidacy, he believed, changed the scale of values. He was deeply disturbed about the Senator's continuing opposition to the Civil Rights Bill and his thinly-veiled appeals to racists, North and South. In the face of "the most crucial and critical election in the history of the nation," King abandoned his neutrality and came down hard on the side of Lyndon Baines Johnson, the Democratic Presidential candidate. Later, at a press conference in Berlin, King said he saw "danger signs of Hitlerism in the candidacy of Mr. Goldwater," adding: "I think the fight for justice will be greatly affected by the American election if Senator Goldwater gets elected President of the United States. I am absolutely convinced we will see a dark night of social disruption and this would so intensify the discontent, the frustration and the despair of the disinherited of our nation, the poverty-stricken people of our nation, many Negroes of our nation, that outbreaks of violence and riots would exist on a scale we have never seen before. This is not in any way to advocate this and it is not to make the prediction of it an invitation to it. But I am stating an actual fact. . . ." To prevent what he considered a clear and present danger to free institutions, King assumed the unfamiliar role of a political campaigner, barnstorming through the North and South for the Democratic ticket. In a desperate attempt to confuse the issues, Republican strategists distributed last-minute leaflets urging Negroes to vote for King as a write-in candidate for President. In an election eve press conference, King denounced this effort as "a cruel and vicious attempt to confuse Negro voters." Urging Negroes to vote for Johnson, he said: "I am not a candidate; please do not vote for me." The decisive repudiation of Goldwater reaffirmed King's faith in the essential soundness of the

In Berlin, King and traveling companion, the Rev. Mr. Abernathy, talk to West Berlin Protestant leaders, including Lutheran Bishop Otto Dibelius (2nd fr. r.). King addressed crowd of twenty thousand Germans in the Waldbühne, a West Berlin amphitheater

West Berlin Mayor Willy Brandt watches as King signs Golden Guest Book at City Hall. King was principal speaker at opening of West Berlin Festival, which was held as a memorial to late President Kennedy.

Bishop Dibelius lauds King at ceremony in the
Dibelius home. Honorary degree of doctor of theology
was conferred on American Protestant leader by
Bishop Dibelius.

King and Abernathy are photographed at Berlin wall. Visit to wall followed reception at Tempelhof Airport by West Berlin Senator Werner Stein and West Berlin Protestant leaders.

Looking into East Berlin, King reflects on "man-made barriers." Despite barriers, he said, "there is something that unites us all as Christians."

Behind Iron Curtain in East Berlin's famous Marienkirche (St. Mary's Church), King, aided by interpreter, addresses overflow crowd. Before his sermon, church choir sang in German and English, "Let My People Go." King told Germans that "the Negro has been called upon to be the conscience of our nation." He also delivered sermon at East Berlin's Sophienkirche.

American people, but it was a bad omen, he said, that so conservative a man was nominated and that twenty-six million Americans voted for him.

In this same period, King became a presence in the international community. In September, on the invitation of Berlin Mayor Willy Brandt, he spoke at a memorial concert for the late President Kennedy. At the urging of West Berlin Protestant leaders, he also crossed the Berlin wall and delivered a sermon at Marienkirche, the city's oldest Protestant church. From Berlin, King and his traveling companion, the Rev. Mr. Abernathy, flew to Rome for a special audience with Pope Paul VI. The two religious leaders were alone for twenty minutes in the Pope's private library in the Vatican's Apostolic Palace. King and the Pope discussed race, religion, and the moral crisis. The Pope, King said later, was well-informed on the American racial problem. King added: "He said he was a friend of the Negro people and that he was following our struggle in the United States." The Pope, according to King, also promised to make a personal and public declaration against racial injustice. Abernathy joined the conference for the last five minutes. At the conclusion of the audience, the Pope gave King a silver medallion commemorating the Second Vatican Council and asked him "to keep in contact." He also asked King to send him copies of his last two books. King was encouraged by the meeting which he said was a "profound encouragement for all Christians in the world and particularly in the United States who are involved in the civil rights struggle with us."

After a short vacation in Madrid, King returned to America where shortly before October 14 he was informed privately that he had been selected as the Nobel Peace Prize winner of 1964. Completely exhausted, uneasily aware of the flood of attention that would now roll over him, and somewhat dazed by the enormity of the thing, King entered Atlanta's St. Joseph Infirmary where he was resting on October 14 when the following announcement was released in Oslo.

> The Nobel Committee of the Norwegian National Assembly has decided to award the Peace Prize for 1964 to Martin Luther King, Jr. The sum of the prize is 283,000 Swedish Kronors [$54,-600].

The committee did not, as usual, announce the basis for the award, which is given annually to the person "who has done most for the furtherance of brotherhood among men and to the abolishment or reduction of standing armies and for the extension of these purposes." The selection of King indicated, among other things, an unprecedented degree of international concern over America's racial struggle. King was the third Negro, the twelfth American, and the youngest person to receive the award since Alfred Nobel instituted it in 1895. Previous Negro winners were Ralph J. Bunche, the UN official who won the 1950 prize for his work in arranging an Arab-Israeli truce in the Palestine war; and Albert Luthuli, former leader of the African National Congress, who received the 1960 award.

Reaction to the selection of King ranged from jubilant applause by many Americans to bitter criticism by segregationists. Telegrams and letters by the hundreds poured into King's Atlanta headquarters. Ralph J. Bunche, a previous winner, sounded the dominant note. "This announcement," he said, "is a striking international recognition of the cause and struggle of the American Negro for full equality in the American society and for full participation in the mainstream of American life." Robert F. Kennedy, the former attorney general, said that the prize was "richly deserved" and that King's life and work symbolized "the struggle of mankind for justice and equality through non-violent means." Former King antagonists like Eugene (Bull) Connor expressed the minority view. "They're scraping the bottom of the barrel," Connor said, "when they pick him. He's caused more strife and trouble in this country than anyone I can think of."

Typically modest and self-effacing, King saw the award as a tribute to his nonviolent followers and "as a sign that world public opinion was on the side of those struggling for freedom and dignity." From his hospital room, King announced that "every penny" of the prize money would go into the civil rights movement. He added, in a prepared statement:

> This is an extremely moving moment in my life. The notice that I have received the 1964 Nobel Prize for Peace is as great a shock for me as was the news of my nomination some months ago. It fills me with deep humility and gratitude to know that I have been chosen as the recipient of this foremost of earthly honors.

Presentation of Nobel Peace Prize medal and scroll is made to Dr. King on December 10, 1964, by Gunnar Jahn, chairman, Nobel Committee of Norwegian Parliament. Dr. King is twelfth American, third Negro, to win the coveted Prize.

After receiving Prize, Dr. King delivers five-minute acceptance speech to largest crowd ever assembled for Peace Prize ceremony in Festival Hall of The University of Oslo. Seated in center aisle are King Olav V and Crown Prince Harald of Norway.

Nobel Peace Prize medal and scroll (left) were presented to Dr. King in public ceremony, while check for 273,000 Swedish kronor ($56,400) was simply brought to hotel room.

A kiss from his wife, Coretta, brings smile to face of Nobel laureate. In foreground are his aide, Rev. Bernard Lee (l.) and close associate, Rev. Ralph D. Abernathy.

I do not consider this merely an honor to me personally, but a tribute to the discipline, wise restraint, and majestic courage of the millions of gallant Negro and white persons of good will who have followed a nonviolent course in seeking to establish a reign of justice and a rule of love across this nation of ours. It is also gratifying to know that the nations of the world recognize the civil rights movement in this country as so significant a moral force as to merit such recognition.

I am sure that it will give me new courage and determination to carry on in this fight to overcome the evils and injustice in this society.

The presentation of this award also brings with it a demand for deepening one's commitment to nonviolence as a philosophy of life and reminds us that we have only begun to explore the powerful spiritual and moral resources which are possible through this way of life. We are also challenged to face the international implications of nonviolence for we know that there can be no justice in our society unless there is peace in the world.

There remained only the ceremonies of recognition in Oslo, the words to be said there, the applause to be heard there, and the sweat and struggle that lay beyond the crest of the hill.

The Nobel Laureate returned from Oslo and plunged into a crucial voter registration campaign in the Black Belt of Alabama. On Sunday, March 7, 1955, King's lieutenants and John Lewis of SNCC began a Selma-to-Montgomery March to protest the slaying of Jimmie Lee Jackson, a black civil rights worker, and the arrest of almost one thousand demonstrators. As the five hundred marchers crossed Selma's Edmund Pettus Bridge, two hundred state troopers and sheriff's deputies lobbed canisters of tear gas and waded in with nightsticks and whips. The brutal scene, as witnessed later that day by millions of TV-viewers, traumatized the nation and sent thousands of blacks and whites to Selma for a pivotal national campaign. During the course of this struggle, three white Unitarian ministers, including the Rev. James J. Reeb, were attacked and beaten. Reeb died later in a Birmingham hospital.

The Selma campaign dramatized King's role as a catalyst of the Christian church. Thousands of priests, nuns, and rabbis flocked to Selma and placed themselves under the direct orders of Martin Luther King. Harvey Cox said later that the Selma experience was crucial in deepening the sensitivity of the white Christian church. He wrote: "When the Roman Catholic archbishop of Birmingham and Mobile, Thomas J. Toolen, told the nuns and priests who were marching in Selma to go home and tend to 'God's business,' they not only refused to go but 300 of them signed a press statement spelling out their dissatisfaction with the archbishop and stating that they would return to Selma, or to other racial crisis spots, whenever Martin Luther King asked them to. Here is a situation without parallel in the history of the Church. Some 300 Roman Catholic clergy refuse to obey a bishop's request and, at the same time, pledge obedience to a Baptist minister who ironically bears the name of the main leader of the Protestant Reformation." (King became a *de facto* Catholic bishop in Selma.)

The events in Selma generated a national pressure President Johnson could not ignore. He told a nationally televised press conference that "what happened in Selma was an American tragedy." Later, on March 15, he went before a rare joint evening session of Congress and called for immediate passage of voting rights legislation. It was during this address that President Johnson adopted Martin Luther King's theme song, saying: "The efforts of American Negroes to secure for themselves the full blessings of American life . . . must be our cause too. Because it's not just for Negroes, but really it's all of us, who must overcome the crippling legacy of bigotry and injustice."

Two days later, a federal court upheld the right of King to stage a fifty-mile march from Selma to Montgomery. When Alabama Governor George Wallace announced that he could not protect the marchers, President Johnson federalized the Alabama National Guard and dispatched a contingent of U.S. troops. Protected by the armed might of America, King and thousands of demonstrators began the second Montgomery march on Sunday, March 21, and ended four days later with a nationally televised rally on the steps of the Alabama state capitol. Largely as a result of this King-led demonstration, the U.S. Congress passed a voting rights bill which authorized the President to suspend literacy tests and send federal examiners into Black Belt counties to register black voters. The net effect was to return the South in a limited sense to the Reconstruction era. Soon, tens of thousands of blacks were registered and a handful of black men and women were sitting in the legislatures and the county courthouses of Dixie.

Epilogue

There was an air of inevitability about it.

First there was the rain, then the snow, then the blood.

Blood called to blood, and there was a convulsion of coast-to-coast violence unprecedented in the civil history of America.

In more than one hundred cities, black people exploded in rebellion.

Ten thousand plate glass windows were broken.

A thousand fires blazed.

Federal troops were deployed to protect the White House and the U.S. Capitol.

There was irony in this.

Martin Luther King, Jr., was a man of peace and nonviolence—and in the first five days after his death, forty-three men, women, and children died in his name.

After the screams, after the smashing of idols, after the purification of fire, there was a funeral in a red-brick Atlanta church, smelling of chrysanthemums and liles, and the rhythmic benediction of a Baptist choir and, out in the audience, women in black, their eyes red from weeping, and the powerful and the famous sitting and standing shoulder to shoulder with the meek and the unknown.

It was a funeral the likes of which has never been seen in this land.

One has to go back ten decades, back to the traveling Lincoln bier, to find an analogue to the marching King catafalque and the rivers of people following his body in misery.

A half-million people were in and of and around this funeral.

Tens of thousands filed past his bier, weeping.

Hundreds of thousands followed the plain wagon and the two Georgia mules which bore him to a second service amid the azaleas and the dogwoods—the crucifixion flower—on the campus of his alma mater, Morehouse College.

Late in the afternoon, when the shadows were long on the new grass, it ended for Martin Luther King, Jr., in the silence of a crypt on a hillside in South View Cemetery.

Something within him had known that it would come to this, to the chrysanthemums and crowds and silence. He had foreseen it all, had thought about it, the weight and the sound and the feel of his own funeral—the long lines and the tears and the immortal silence of a closed casket on the other side of the world.

Something deep inside him *knew*.

But nothing inside him or outside him, neither the snow nor the rain nor the thunder and lightning, warned him against the specific web the spider of racism was spinning in the last days of his life.

When, on Lincoln's birthday, the garbage workers went out on strike, he was far away, deep in plans for tomorrows that would never come. All that day—February 12, 1968—he sat in his Atlanta office planning for April days he would not see. Two months before, in December, 1967, he had announced plans to go to Washington, to the seat of Caesar, with a Poor People's Campaign; and now, in Memphis, he was closeted with aides in an all-day strategy session. In this meeting, King and his aides made plans for every contingency, save one. They decided what they would do in Washington in April if X did Y and how they would respond if Y did X. They decided many things of moment, but they did not decide what they would do about the garbage workers, who were going out on strike now in Memphis, Tennessee.

This strike grew out of an earlier decision, which was made in the rain. Because of the rain, which fell on Memphis on January 31, city officials made a decision which would lead, web by web, to the martyrdom of Martin Luther King, Jr. They didn't plan it that way. But a pattern of racism, as old as the slave ships which brought King's ancestors to this country, worked in them and through them. It was this pattern which spun the first web of death. It was this pattern which led Memphis officials to separate garbage collectors on the basis of race, sending the black workers home with two hours pay and keeping the white men for a full day's work. This decision, which would change so many lives, which would lead to so many graves, angered the black garbage collectors who held a meeting and decided to go out on strike. The strike catalyzed the black community of Memphis and sent ripples of red across the land.

The Memphis strike did not immediately engage King's attention. He was involved just then in a struggle for his very existence as a national leader. Although he was still the foremost symbol of the struggle for racial justice, he was being pressed by Stokely Carmichael and Rap Brown and other leaders who stressed Black Power and militant self-defense. More ominously, his moral authority as a champion of nonviolence was being eroded by a new mood rising from the despair and determination of the very young and the very defiant. This new mood was behind the annual summer seasons of riots and rebellions. In 1966, King moved to meet this new challenge by organizing his first Northern campaign in Chicago, Illinois. He rented an apartment in the city, organized tenants' unions, and staged marches which attracted national attention. On one of these marches, angry white racists stoned King and dispersed his supporters. King redoubled his efforts, winning a paper agreement on open housing from Chicago's white power structure. In 1967, he organized a second Northern campaign in Cleveland; but the economic roots of racism resisted his nonviolent approach, and black people, in despair, exploded in rebellion after rebellion. The awesome insurrection of Watts in 1965 was followed by Cleveland and Chicago and scores of other cities in 1966 and and the 1967 cataclysm of Newark and Detroit.

King's Poor People's Campaign was designed, in part, to answer his critics and to reverse the drift toward violence. He planned to take thousands of blacks, Puerto Ricans, and poor whites to the capital and camp there until Congress passed a multi-billion program of national reconstruction. In King's view, the Poor People's Campaign was going to be a litmus test for nonviolence. It was going to prove, once and for all, whether nonviolence could attack the structural roots of racism and provide an alternative to violence. And so, while the garbage collectors of Memphis marched, King crisscrossed the country, seeking resources and bodies for the Washington campaign. During this same period, he moved into the leadership of the forces opposing the Vietnam War, which he considered immoral and irresponsible.

As the calendar moved toward the ides of March, King made a whirlwind People-to-People pilgrimage which takes on new meaning in the light of subsequent events. For what he did now, with no inkling of the unfolding web which was pulling him toward his death, was to make one last triumphant tour of the scenes of his greatest nonviolent campaigns. On Thursday night, February 15, he spoke in Birmingham, the scene of the massive demonstrations of 1963. The next morning, Friday, February 16, he spoke to a large and enthusiastic group in Selma, the focal point of the famous Selma-to-Montgomery March. That same afternoon, he visited Montgomery, where thirteen years before he had started his rise to worldwide acclaim. This eerily meaningful journey into the past gave King new hope and he flew off to Jamaica with his wife Coretta and his aide, Andrew Young, for his final vacation.

By the time King returned to America, the web of fate was tightening. The Memphis garbage strike had moved from the periphery to the center of the civil rights movement, and King decided to lead a mass march in Memphis on March 22. But on that Friday, a massive snowfall blanketed Memphis in a shroud of white. And the march was postponed until Thursday, March 28. On this date King led a march of six thousand protestors. As it turned out, this was one of the major miscalculations of King's life. For, as he himself later admitted, the march was poorly planned and insufficiently monitored. Worse, King committed his name to a venture over which he had little control. This became apparent soon after the march began. Young militants, disdainful of King's methods, broke away and started smashing windows and looting stores. Within a few minutes, a full-scale riot was under way, and National Guardsmen were rushed to the city. Before the turbulence subsided, one person had been killed and sixty-two had been injured.

King missed the excitement. When the rioting began, his aides, fearful for his life, pushed him into a passing car and sped to the Rivermont Motel on the banks of the Mississippi. Here, in a posh and depressingly white setting, King, who had less than a week to live, spent what one of his associates later called the worst night of his life.

Outside the Rivermont, men were saying that Martin Luther King, Jr., the apostle of nonviolence, had led a march that degenerated into violence. Some men were demanding cancellation of the projected Poor People's Campaign in Washington. Others were saying that it was all over for King, that history had passed him by.

Inside the Rivermont, King studied the reports and lapsed into an intense depression which lasted, his aides say, for most of the last week of his life. Jesse Jackson, a top King aide, said, "Some of us didn't understand, and he was going through this extreme tension; he was in the Garden of Gethsemane, making a decision trying to see which way to go." Chauncey Eskridge, King's tax consultant and personal advisor, said: "He could agonize himself so. He couldn't help feeling that agony. Riots depressed him, and he would say that it was his fault. He would ask himself, 'Am I doing any good?' " Rev. Ralph Abernathy, who was with King throughout that terrible night, said later: "I had never seen him so depressed." According to Abernathy, King spoke of the possibility of going on a personal retreat for meditation and reflection. Jesse Jackson says King spoke of the possibility of imitating Gandhi by going on a prolonged fast until black people abandoned violence "and the Stokelys and the Raps and the Youngs and the Wilkins united."

King was still in a state of indecision and depression when he flew back to Atlanta on the day after the riot. Rev. Abernathy, King's constant companion and successor, rode with him from the Atlanta airport to the West Side of Atlanta. When the car reached King's home on Sunset Avenue, Abernathy got out and tried to comfort his friend. He suggested a movie or a session at the health club of the Butler Street YMCA. King shook Abernathy off. He was in no mood for diversions. "I'll pull out of it, Ralph," Abernathy recalls King saying. "I might call you later on."

Later that night, King and his wife dined at the Abernathys. They had an entrée of pig ears and pig feet and a main course of fried kroker fish. The soul food, King's favorite, revived his spirit; and the two couples sat up until the wee hours of the morning, joshing and whiling away the time.

The next day, Saturday, March 30, King called a staff meeting in the pastor's study at Ebenezer Baptist Church. But he seemed somehow detached from the proceedings. He sat on the edge of the group and, at one point, denounced the tensions and dissensions within the staff. According to Abernathy, he said: "Before we can go to Washington, something has to happen within this staff." Jesse Jackson has a similar recollection of this crucial staff meeting. "I had never seen him under such a spiritual cloud before," he said. "He talked with us and at one point he left the meeting because he didn't feel the staff was as intellectually and as spiritually involved in the Washington project as we should have been. . . . He was calling the roll, just going around the room until he got all of us to feeling bad. Then he left. . . ." Abernathy followed King out of the meeting. "I didn't like the way he was acting," Abernathy said later. "I was worried about him. But he told me he would be all right and said: 'I'll pull out of it, Ralph.'"

King pulled out of it; so did the staff. Within a few minutes after King's departure, the staff was caught up in an extraordinary emotional fervor which led to a number of concrete proposals. The most important of these proposals was that it was necessary for Dr. King to go to Washington with the Poor People's Campaign, but that it was necessary for him to go by way of Memphis. This idea was relayed to King by staff members who told him that it was important for him to return to the meeting. "Doc," one staff member said, "The Holy Spirit is in this room." King returned to the meeting and decided to turn disaster into triumph by going to Memphis and proving that nonviolence was not dead.

King had, at that point, only five days to live. At some point within these five days, according to close associates, he transcended the agony of doubt and reached a new plateau of understanding and acceptance. "The ordeal," Chauncey Eskridge said, "strengthened him." Jesse Jackson said, "He made the decision after he saw the mountain there."

The mountain was there waiting, on Wednesday, April 3, when

Martin Luther King, Jr., returned to Memphis to lead a second march. He checked into Room 306—a $12-a-day double room on the second floor of the Lorraine Motel—and went into a series of conferences with lawyers and aides over a court injunction which banned the proposed march. He was still conferring late that afternoon when a tornado roared over the city. Wind from the tornado ripped off roofs, shook windows, and sprayed the city with uncollected garbage. Rain came down in sheets. A local radio personality regarded the natural disaster with foreboding and said on the air: "Maybe, God is trying to tell us something."

The rain came down, lightning rent the sky, thunder spoke—and men and institutions moved with the inexorability of a Greek tragedy toward the eye of a national disaster.

Somewhere in Memphis at that moment, National Guardsmen, who had been on duty since the riot, were returning to their homes to prepare for the Easter season.

Somewhere in Memphis, a white man or a group of white men were studying murder.

Somewhere in Memphis, Martin Luther King's aides were recruiting nonviolent marshals for a march King would never lead.

At that moment, King was regarding the rain with disquiet. He was scheduled to speak at a mass meeting that night and his aides were advising him not to go. The rain, they reasoned, would limit the crowd; and if King spoke to an empty house, reporters would write another spate of stories about the death of nonviolence. King listened to the advisors and decided to send a substitute speaker. But a few minutes later, Ralph Abernathy called King and told him there were two thousand people in Mason Temple and that they wanted to see and hear him.

King put on his coat and went out into the driving rain to deliver the last speech of his life. No one knows really what went on in his mind that night. No one knows why he decided to talk about death. But men sometimes *know* more than they know. And the words, which came from deep within King this night, were words of death; and it would seem twenty-four hours later that he knew precisely what was going to happen and why it was going to happen. He had lived now for a long time in the shadow of death, had the taste of it in his mouth. There had been many attempts on his life and he knew that there would be others and he knew that someday somebody would succeed. He had spoken of these things many times before to intimates. Now he said it out loud, taking the audience into his confidence, telling them about mountains and valleys, about the good days and the bad.

"We've got some difficult days ahead," he said. "But it really doesn't matter with me now. Because I've been to the mountaintop. I won't mind. Like anybody, I would like to live a long life. Longevity has its place. But I'm not concerned about that now. I just want to do God's will. And He's allowed me to go up to the mountain. And I've looked over, and I've seen the Promised Land. I may not get there with you, but I want you to know tonight that we as a people will get to the Promised Land. So I'm happy tonight. I'm not fearing any man. *Mine eyes have seen the glory of the coming of the Lord!*"

King went out into the rain, buoyed up by the cheers of thousands. He spent almost all of the next day—Thursday, April 4—in his room, challenging his staff to live up to the principles of nonviolence.

While he talked, the web tightened around him. Between 3 and 3:30 P.M., a white man slipped into a rooming house on a rise overlooking the motel. He had binoculars and a rifle. He took up a position in the common bathroom facing Room 306—and he waited.

When King emerged from his room to go to dinner, he was centered in the cross-hairs of the telescopic sight of a high-powered rifle. King tarried for a moment in the eye of death. He leaned over the green railing of the balcony and chatted with aides on the ground below. As he started to straighten up, a shot rang out. He fell backwards, blood flowing from gaping wounds in his right jaw and neck.

There was an icy moment of silence, then a woman screamed for all her life.

King lay on the walkway concrete, his legs propped up on the railing, his eyes wide open. He did not speak; and apparently he did not suffer. The single bullet severed his spinal cord. He died at 7:02 P.M. in St. Joseph's Hospital at the age of thirty-nine.

Now began the rites of martyrdom, the eulogies and memorials, the riots and the tears.

Now began the unprecedented tributes, the postponement of the baseball season, the shutting down of the docks, the lowering of all U.S. flags to half-staff.

Now began the marches which extended from one end of the country to the other and ended five days later on Tuesday, April 9, 1968, when Martin Luther King, Jr., was laid to rest in an Atlanta cemetery green with new grass and the promise of new life.

It is true, as Carl Sandburg has so eloquently said, that "a tree is measured best when it is down." And in April, in the Easter Season, when the tall, young tree fell in the United States of America, men vied with each other in describing its size.

The World Council of Churches said King was one of the first citizens of the world.

Paul Douglas, former U.S. Senator, said King ranked with Gandhi and Pope John as outstanding religious leaders of the century.

William Stringfellow said that future historians will call him "the best friend the white American ever had."

And Benjamin E. Mays, in an eloquent eulogy, said King was "called of God," adding: "If Amos and Micah were prophets in the eighth century B.C., Martin Luther King, Jr. was a prophet in the twentieth century. If Isaiah was called of God to prophesy in his day, Martin Luther was called of God to prophesy in his day. If Hosea was sent to preach love and forgiveness centuries ago, Martin Luther was sent to expound the doctrine of nonviolence and forgiveness in the third quarter of the twentieth century."

In the Niagara of tributes, King's voice was heard. In a sense, one can say that he preached his own funeral. For at the private services at Ebenezer Baptist Church, a tape was played of the sermon he had preached at Ebenezer on Sunday, February 4, 1968. In this sermon, King said:

If any of you are around when I have to meet my day, I don't want a long funeral. And if you get somebody to deliver the eulogy, tell him not to talk too long. . . . Tell them not to mention that I have a Nobel Peace Prize. That isn't important. Tell them not to mention that I have three or four hundred other awards. That's not important. Tell them not to mention where I went to school. I'd like somebody to mention that day, that Martin Luther King, Jr. tried to give his life serving others. I'd like for somebody to say that day, that Martin Luther King, Jr. tried to love somebody. I want you to say that day that I tried to be right on the war question. I want you to be able to say that day, that I did try to feed the hungry. And I want you to be able to say that day that I did try in my life to clothe those who were naked. I want you to say on that day, that I did try in my life to visit those who were in prison. I want you to say that I tried to love and serve humanity.

All this—and more—was said of Martin Luther King, Jr. on the day of his interment. And men will undoubtedly say for years to come that he was an exemplary servant of humanity. For, in death as in life, King bypassed cerebral centers and attacked the archetypal roots of man. His grace, like Gandhi's, grew out of a complicated relation not to oppression but to the ancient scourges of man, to pain, to suffering, to death. Men who conquer the fear of these things in themselves acquire extraordinary power over themselves and over others.

"A man who won't die for something," King said, "is not fit to live."

By resurrecting that truth and flinging it into the teeth of our fears, by saying it repeatedly and by living it, Martin Luther King, Jr. taught us, all of us, black men and white men, Jews and Gentiles, not only how to die, but also, and more importantly, how to live.

RECORD OF ARRESTS

January 26, 1956.   Arrested, Montgomery, Alabama, on charge of traveling thirty miles an hour in twenty-five mile zone. Released on recognizance bond.

January 28, 1956.   Fined $10 in Montgomery police court on not-guilty plea on traffic charge.

February 21, 1956.   Indicted with other leading figures of Montgomery Bus Boycott on charge of being party to a conspiracy to hinder and prevent operation of a business without "just or legal cause."

February 23, 1956.   Booked at Montgomery jail on indictment and released on $300 bond.

March 22, 1956.   Convicted after four-day trial in Montgomery Circuit Court on February 21 indictment. Fine of $500 suspended pending appeal which was not perfected within allotted time by King's attorneys. King paid fine finally under complicated arrangement under which charges against other boycott leaders and a group of white segregationists were dropped.

September 3, 1958.	Arrested on charge of loitering (later changed to failure to obey an officer) in vicinity of Montgomery Recorder's Court. Released on $100 bond.
September 4, 1958.	Convicted after not-guilty plea on charge of failure to obey an officer. Fourteen dollars fine paid almost immediately—over King's objections—by Montgomery Police Commissioner Clyde C. Sellers.
February 17, 1960.	Arrested in Atlanta on Alabama warrant following his indictment by Montgomery County Grand Jury on two counts of perjury in connection with the filing of 1956 and 1958 state income tax returns. Released on $2,000 bond.
May, 1960.	Arrested, DeKalb County, Georgia, on charge of driving without valid Georgia driver's license. Released on bond.
May 28, 1960.	Acquitted by jury of twelve white men in Montgomery Circuit Court of charges of falsely swearing to information on 1956 state income tax return. Second count of indictment (see February 17, 1960) was later dropped.
September 23, 1960.	Paid $25 fine and received twelve-month probated sentence after guilty plea in DeKalb County court on May, 1960, traffic violation.
October 19, 1960.	Arrested in Atlanta, Georgia, sit-in; jailed on charge of violating state's anti-trespass law.
October 22, 1960.	Sit-in charges dropped; all demonstrators except King released. King was ordered held on charge of violating probated sentence in traffic case (see September 23, 1960).
October 25, 1960.	Transferred from Fulton County jail to DeKalb County jail in Decatur, an Atlanta suburb.
October 25, 1960.	Sentenced to four months in jail by DeKalb County judge who ruled that his participation in sit-in violated terms of his probated traffic sentence.
October 26, 1960.	Transferred to Reidsville State Prison.
October 27, 1960.	Released from Reidsville State Prison on $2,000 appeal bond.

March 7, 1961.	Georgia Court of Appeals remanded traffic case to DeKalb County on grounds that original sentence should not have exceeded six months.
April 8, 1961.	Received $25 fine and suspended six-month sentence on original traffic case (see September 23, 1960) in DeKalb County court.
December 16, 1961.	Arrested in Albany, Georgia, demonstration on charge of obstructing sidewalk and parading without permit.
December 18, 1961.	Released on bail in truce that later collapsed.
July 10, 1962.	Convicted in Albany (Ga.) Recorder's Court of violating street and sidewalk ordinance by leading parade without permit on December 16, 1961. Received sentence of $178 or forty-five days in jail. Entered jail to serve forty-five day term.
July 12, 1962.	Released against his will after $178 fine was paid by mystery man.
July 27, 1962.	Arrested in Albany city hall "prayer vigil" and jailed on charges of failure to obey police officer, obstructing sidewalk and disorderly conduct.
August 10, 1962.	Convicted, Albany Recorder's Court, and placed on sixty-day probation for July 27 vigil. Released from jail.
April 12, 1963.	Arrested in Birmingham, Alabama on charges of parading without a permit and contempt of court
April 20, 1963.	Released from Birmingham jail on $300 cash bond.
June 11, 1964.	Arrested in St. Augustine, Florida, sit-in on charge of violating state's anti-trespass law.
June 13, 1964.	Released on $300 bond.

PHOTOGRAPHIC CREDITS

INDEX

MAR 2104

MAR   2004